# Superstar
# Customer Service

# SUPERSTAR CUSTOMER SERVICE

### A 31-Day Plan to Improve Client Relations, Lock in New Customers, and Keep the Best Ones Coming Back for More

## RICK CONLOW
*and*
## DOUG WATSABAUGH

CAREER
PRESS

Pompton Plains, NJ

SUPERSTAR CUSTOMER SERVICE
EDITED BY JODI BRANDON
TYPESET BY EILEEN MUNSON
Cover design by Jeff Piasky
Printed in the U.S.A.

To order this title, please call toll-free 1-800-CAREER-1 (NJ and Canada: 201-848-0310) to order using VISA or MasterCard, or for further information on books from Career Press.

The Career Press, Inc.
220 West Parkway, Unit 12
Pompton Plains, NJ 07444
www.careerpress.com

**Library of Congress Cataloging-in-Publication Data**

Conlow, Rick.
  Superstar customer service : a 31-day plan to improve client relations, lock in new customers, and keep the best ones coming back for more / Rick Conlow, Doug Watsabaugh.
      pages cm
  ISBN 978-1-60163-276-0 (pbk.) -- ISBN 978-1-60163-518-1 (ebook) 1. Customer services. 2. Customer relations. I. Watsabaugh, Doug, 1951- II. Title.

HF5415.5.C654 2014
958.8'12--dc23

2013036050

# CONTENTS

# INTRODUCTION

*Superstar Customer Service* is the third in a three part series focused on **Superstar Performance** written by Rick Conlow and Doug Watsabaugh of WCW Partners. The books are published by Career Press and are aimed straight at achieving *the highest levels of performance in leadership, sales, and customer service.*

WCW Partners has been in the consulting business for nearly two decades and has consistently proven that we are all capable of achieving unlimited possibilities if we believe in ourselves and if we continuously seek new skills and knowledge. In the March 1, 2013, issue of *Inc.* magazine, Kevin Daum wrote an article entitled "10 Things *Really* Amazing Employees Do." In his article, Daum describes 10 very insightful things employees can do to help a business succeed, and then he offers guidance on what management can do to help.[1] We like that Daum addressed himself directly to the employees and described the very important role that they play in making a business successful. And, he provided guidance to the leadership on what they need to do to facilitate the success of the employees. Our approach is similar. Here is the premise behind *Superstar Customer Service.*

## About *Superstar Customer Service*

This book is written to help front-line employees realize you can be a Superstar customer service provider. You may have one of the most demanding and difficult jobs you'll ever have and, even then, it has the potential to make you a Superstar!

Develop your skills, manage yourself, and master your ability to address the relationship problems experienced by your company, and you can go anywhere you want to go. Job satisfaction, success, and personal accomplishment are all in your grasp. This book is organized as a month-long journey of improvement and discovery. Each chapter is a "daily lesson" with a core concept, skill development idea, and resources to support your practice and application of the lesson. If you read and use this book, you will improve your ability to provide Superstar service in your company. You will distinguish yourself as someone who can get things done, and you may very well begin a new pathway in your career success that is far beyond anything that you have previously imagined! There are several ways you can use this book:

1. Read it alone and use it as a "seminar in a box." Use the tools, the Superstar Customer Service Self-Assessment, and the Interpretation and Action Planning Guide, and the application and development planning tools to build your skills and mastery leading to increasing success.

2. Read it with your team. Many leadership teams that we work with read books and discuss them together much as a book club would do. Their purpose it to deepen their understanding and application of leadership skills and knowledge together for the benefit of the business. You can offer *Superstar Customer Service* as a team learning tool with your supervisor and service team. By reading a daily concept and discussing it as a team, you can support one another's development and improve your team's skills together.

3. *Superstar Customer Service* can be used as a seminar or training program, facilitated by a professional trainer or by a service manager. The program can be broken into a 31-day offering, or the content can be grouped into weekly sessions, each covering five to seven daily lessons with a review discussion as the next week's session begins.

4. The daily lessons can be used as content to start or end regular staff meetings so that the department manager facilitates ongoing training over a series of 31 meetings covering a time span chosen by the manager.

5. Many teams are geographically dispersed across the United States or across the world. It is challenging to maintain a common focus and consistent message when huge distances separate us. *Superstar Customer Service* can be used to offer and reinforce a common set of skills and a common culture of service throughout your service network. Whether offered during a web conference or teleconference, *Superstar Customer Service* can be used to offer a short content message, followed by an individual follow-through assignment from each participant's individual copy of the book.

There are many other ways you may find this book useful. First and foremost, we encourage you to read it, get involved with it, and apply it to your job and your life. We are certain that you will find it beneficial in your current job and in support of your long-term career direction. We wish you success on your journey and we hope to read about your Superstar service success in the future.

P.S.: We want thank our partner and communication specialist Alyssa MacDowell for her invaluable and tireless efforts in helping us write, edit, and improve this book. She is a true superstar!

> *Customer service is just a day in, day*
> *out, ongoing, never ending, unremitting,*
> *persevering, compassionate type of activity.*
> —Leon Gorman, CEO, L.L.Bean

## Beginnings Are Prophetic
### *The Power of Knowing Your Role in Your Organization*

Imagine a world without customer service. You wake up in the middle of the night because it's cold in your house. There's no heat coming from the furnace. You grab your cell phone to call the energy company, but the tower that services your area is inactive. Both companies have cut power to save money. There is no one to which you can call and complain.

Let's say you go to the grocery store, grab a cart, and start walking down the aisles. You find that some of the shelves have food but some don't. After searching for help, you finally come across a store employee who is sitting on a bench, having a smoke. You ask, "Can you help me?" The person responds by asking, "What makes you so special?"

On your way home, you stop to get gas. It's a self-help station, of course. As your tank approaches full capacity, the pump malfunctions and gas begins to spill all over the ground. You run into the station for help, but the store clerk irately declares you to be at fault before threatening to call the police. You end up paying extra to cover the cost of the cleanup and wasted gas so that you can avoid further escalating the situation.

Later, you stop at a restaurant for dinner. The hostess eyes you suspiciously and says, "You better pay your bill. Go seat yourself." You order a meal, but when your drink arrives you realize that it's not what you had ordered. The waitress never returns to your table and you're forced to flag down another one to help. She tells you to wait your turn for service. Shortly thereafter, a man lumbers over to your table and begrudgingly slides your overcooked dinner in front of you and says, "No more complaints from you. Eat your meal, pay for it, and get out."

A world with a complete disregard for customer service, as this scenario demonstrates, can leave customers feeling victimized. Consumers who feel mistreated in this way are significantly less likely to invest capital in a store or corporation if they feel that even their most basic service needs aren't being met. Stories of substandard customer service travel quickly in the age of social media, and companies that may not have incurred any public relations damage a decade ago are much more susceptible to bad press today.

The words *customer service* imply a degree of support to consumers who have already invested money into a business or who may do so in the future. All jobs require customer service at three levels:

1. **Product.** It needs to perform as promised.

2. **Price.** It needs to be honored as advertised.

3. **People.** People need to interact with customers in a helpful and courteous manner.

If the quality of the product or the accuracy of the price is in question, employees—the customer service representatives—must resolve the issue. If the customer needs assistance in selecting a product, a sales-oriented employee must be able to offer help. The competition is destined to overtake a company that lacks strong customer service. As a result, employees who work at the point-of-sale and can't deliver basic customer service are expendable. The better a company services its customers, the higher its potential for long-term growth. High customer satisfaction stands to benefit the employees themselves in the form of salary increases and promotions due to their good work. The fate of both the company and its employees is closely intertwined with the quality of its customer service. The following data outline the benefits of customer service[1].

Businesses that have poorer ratings in customer service:

▶ Charge prices that are only 98 percent of their competitors.

▶ Lose 2 percent market share.

▶ Have 1 percent profitability on sales.

▶ Grow at an average rate of 8 percent.

Businesses that have higher ratings in customer service:

▶ Charge prices 107 percent higher than their competitors.

▶ Gain 6 percent market share.

▶ Have 12 percent profitability on sales.

▶ Grow at an average rate of 17 percent.

What does this mean for you? No matter which position you hold within a company, a focus on customer service offers your greatest chance for success. Some jobs require a more specialized focus. For example, occupations that involve developing the product, such as an aircraft mechanic, technical illustrator, pipefitter, or web designer, require a different level of customer service. They typically involve relatively little interaction with the public or customers, but the quality of their work still directly affects a company's customer service. A poor-quality product draws in poor press and lessens customer loyalty, whereas an excellent product can overcome a lackluster point-of-sale interaction and create a long-term customer. For example, Lincoln, Lexus, and Toyota are car manufacturers whose products have set the standard within the automobile industry and garner a certain degree of customer satisfaction due to their high-quality, reliable vehicles.

Other employee positions may deal with the public and provide direct customer service on a more regular basis. For example, in positions like flight attendants, retail sales clerks, administrative assistants, and waitresses or waiters, an impersonal employee will drive people away. Friendly, courteous, and helpful service draws customers back. Southwest Airlines' flight attendants have an excellent reputation within their industry due to their high quality of customer service. In the retail arena, Wegmans grocery chain and Nordstrom set the bar for going above and beyond for their customers.

The role of any position can be classified in two ways. **External roles** involve working directly with the customer on the phone, online, or in person. These employees serve as the interface between the company and the consumer. **Internal roles** support other employees who work within the first role to some degree. People in internal roles often forget the impact they can have on the paying customer. Their customer is their fellow employee on the front line. Within these two roles, teamwork is essential to successful customer service for any company. Think about it. If you're a manager within a company and always treat other managers or employees with disdain for their mistakes or shortcomings, you are contributing to an oppressive work environment. It can be easy for a belittled or unsatisfied employee working in this environment to allow this kind of atmosphere to negatively affect the relationships with their customers, thus driving customers to look for better customer service elsewhere.

Your understanding of both the importance of customer service and your role as it relates to the consumer is crucial to your success as an employee. The results of your work directly contribute to your company's reputation and success or failure every day. Beginnings are often prophetic because if you don't know or don't care what your role is from the start, a miserable outcome will likely follow. If you know your role and want to do well, you can expect a more promising outcome.

If you don't fully understand what is expected of you, ask a coworker for clarification. Better yet, grab a sheet of paper and write down the top three to five activities on which you think you are being evaluated. Be as specific as possible. Next, write three to five questions pertaining to those activities that you would like clarified. Then go to your supervisor and request to review it with him or her in person. Few employees ever do things like this, but it builds confidence in both the employee and the employer. Most managers will be delighted. Why? Because you've demonstrated care, competence, and initiative, which are traits of a Superstar employee.

To be a Superstar customer service representative you must perform your role with care, treating the internal and external customer with dignity, respect, and humility. You must also give great consideration to the correctness, completeness, and quality of the technical aspects of your position. Employees who remain diligent in fulfilling these aspects of their job will find themselves faced with more career advancement opportunities, as well as higher salaries, than coworkers who were hired for similar positions. Who could say no to that?

> *A customer is the most important visitor*
> *on our premises, he is not dependent on*
> *us. We are dependent on him. He is not an*
> *interruption in our work. He is the purpose*
> *of it. He is not an outsider in our business.*
> *He is part of it. We are not doing him a*
> *favor by serving him. He is doing us a favor*
> *by giving us an opportunity to do so.*
> —Mahatma Gandhi

## What's My Job? What's Expected of Me? Why Am I Important?

On many occasions at work, you may feel like you wear many proverbial hats. One moment you are helping a customer find the perfect birthday present for his or her child, the next moment you are playing resident IT expert, troubleshooting the error message on your boss's computer, and the next you may feel like the resident janitor, picking up after coworkers in the break room. Often, your perceived roles and responsibilities become so many that it is easy to lose sight of what you were initially hired for. To start on the road to becoming a Superstar customer service representative, it is important to define your role and identify what your job is all about. Though other impromptu roles, like IT expert or garbage disposal specialist may arise, identifying and improving upon the fundamental roles of your position will not only make you a better employee, but will also help when it comes to raises and promotions in the future.

To identify your position's roles, it is best to go back to basics. When you were hired, one of the first things you probably did was review your job duties and goals with your manager. Take a moment to remember what this conversation entailed or, better yet, get a copy of your original job description. If you don't have one, ask your manager to define one for you. Why is this important? Our experience with our clients shows that nearly 80 percent of performance problems on the job are because of the lack of clear expectations and goals. Then, make a plan to do this job review process monthly or quarterly. Not only will it keep you grounded in the fundamental definitions of your job, it will also help improve communication, problem-solving, goal clarity, and motivation between you and your boss.

Knowing the ins and outs of your role is essential for success in the workplace. If you know your role and want to do well, you can expect a promising outcome; maybe you will get a raise or promoted. If you don't, the opposite happens. Your productivity goes down, you don't get as much done, and you could even get fired. If you don't quite understand what is expected of you, take initiative. Define three to five goals, five to seven key duties, and three to five questions that you need clarified or answered about your job. Then, go to your supervisor and ask if you can review it with him or her in person. By letting your supervisor know you want to clarify your job goals, expectations, and action steps, you will show initiative and drive, something few employees ever do. This type of motivation and drive are excellent traits of an employee and lays the foundation for becoming a true Superstar.

## Why You Matter

Employees are among the most important parts of a business. As an employee, you are the face of your company. *You* are the company when you interact with a customer in person, on the phone, by e-mail, or through a text. If the company has a breakdown, *you* make the difference. If you are having a breakdown, how you deal with the situation, good or bad, matters.

Customer service on an employee level is an important asset to every company. Many organizations don't foster an environment that supports their employees in giving good customer service. Without support, it becomes harder to serve the customer well. No matter how difficult it may become, employee-level service is essential in maintaining customer loyalty at your company. Think about the following questions: If your company's product breaks, does the customer care whether you are supported as an employee? If your phone lines are really busy and the customer waited on hold for 10 minutes, does he or she care that the company hasn't worked out a better system? If your customer asks you a question about a new product that you don't know about, does he or she care that you didn't receive proper training? The answer to each of these questions is no. Customers expect what they want or need whether your company is perfect or not. It is your job, regardless of the state of your company, to take care of your customers. No excuses. Superstars understand this; the rest don't.

To be fair to companies, employees can slack off, can be lazy, and don't always do what they are capable of. If you are sick but you go to work anyway and you are moving slowly, the customer doesn't care that you are sick. The customer doesn't care if your coworker is mad at you and you are irritated about it, or if you are frustrated by continuous computer glitches that make your job more difficult. It is still your job, regardless of your state of being, to take care of your customers, because to them, you are the face of the company for that transaction.

You probably don't act like the employees described. As a customer, you know what we are talking about. How many times in the last week or month have you received unsatisfactory service? It happens regularly. In fact, WCW Partners' research suggests that the following are the two biggest reasons people quit being customers:

1. 68 percent leave because of rude, indifferent employees.

2. 14 percent leave because of unresolved complaints.

In total, 82 percent of the time, employees are involved in some way when a customer decides to leave. This goes to show employees, just like the companies they work for, aren't perfect either.

Now, how does this relate to your role and why are you important? Imagine you want to be an Olympic champion. You start working out and begin to get in shape. Your friends notice you are in sweats more often than before. They ask, "What are you doing?" You tell them you are training to be an Olympic champion. They ask, "Where will you be competing?" You say you don't know yet but you will figure it out. They look at you funny and say, "We see you're running, jumping, and doing sit-ups. What sport is that for?" You tell them you haven't decided yet but in time you will.

What are your chances of becoming an Olympic champion? Not good. To be the best, you need to focus and get specific about your role, expectations, and goals. You need to train like an Olympic athlete to be able to perform your best. It's been said that it takes 10,000 hours of practice to win an Olympic medal. That's 50 hours of training a week for four years. To achieve your goal you would need to, among other things, identify your event, determine your best performance in the event, determine the best performances in the world, identify a training regimen to improve, choose events to participate in to gauge your results, outline an appropriate diet, and identify a coach who will help you. All of this requires belief, dedication, and persistence to do what it takes to excel.

## WIFY (What's in It for You)

Excellent customer service benefits more than just the company and the customer. If you focus on delivering Superstar customer service, you will:

▶ Have more confidence and competence in your job.

▶ Develop more pride and job satisfaction in what you do.

▶ Perform better and help customers in a positive manner.

▶ Get more recognition for a job well done.

▶ Realize more opportunities for advancement if you want them.

We have traveled and worked with Superstars from Los Angeles to New York City, Minneapolis/St. Paul to Atlanta, London to Hong Kong, Johannesburg to Sydney, and Vancouver to Montreal. From these experiences, we have learned what the best do and what the worst do and, from this, have adapted fundamental principles for success. The philosophies, principles, and practices shared here will work for you as you learn, internalize, and apply them to your situation and personality, and will help you become the Superstar you have the potential to be.

| Superstar Application: My Customer Service Role |
|---|
| My Goals (3–5) |

| **Superstar Application: My Customer Service Role (continued)** |
| :--- |
| Key Job Priorities (5–7) |
| Questions I Have About My Job |

*Do what you do so well that they will want*
*to see it again and bring their friends.*
—Walt Disney

## How Serious Should I Be About This Work, Anyway?
### Why Should I Care, Really?

Customer service is seriously lacking in most places you spend your money. Think about it: Can you recall a recent experience where the customer service was really poor? Typically, the answer is yes. Think of other places you have been in the last week: a grocery store, a bank, a restaurant, a fast food chain, a department store, a gas station, a hotel, an airline, an online merchant, and so on. How many of these had poor or average service? Probably most. Now think of how many really stood out and had outstanding service. Were there as many? That's part of the problem today; not many people and the businesses they work for really deliver excellent service. Furthermore, most don't seem to know how to or really care about giving good service even if they say they do.

Why is customer service that poor? One reason is that customers have become accustomed to poorer service. They have become numb, tend to ignore poor service, and don't demand anything better. Companies don't help the matter, frequently treating employees as commodities, not valuable resources. Correspondingly, they don't train, coach, or support their employees to do a better job. Of course there are exceptions to this. Wegmans grocery store chain is perennially rated number one in retail across the United States. They treat their employees well, and the employees in turn take care of their customers. In addition, Wegmans' in-store amenities make customers' experiences pleasant, making them feel like a trip to the grocery store is not just another shopping trip. A third consideration is that companies and people don't really believe in delivering better service. They do just enough to get by. If they don't get very good service as customers, why give it to others?

How bad is the state of customer service in the market today? The American Customer Satisfaction Institute (*www.theacsi.org*) at the Ross Business School at the University of Michigan rates some 240 companies across 34 industries on a monthly basis. These ratings are more about the customer service provided by employees than customers' satisfaction with the quality of the product. The average rating is 76.9. If you were a professor grading papers that would be, at best, a C grade. The airline industry has a 67 average, a D+ if you are keeping score, and retail is rated 78, a C average. In total, most companies receive poor to average ratings. After Thomas J. Peters's 1985 book *In Search of Excellence,* discussing the importance of high quality service, was published, companies spent billions of dollars to improve. Most of it made little impact.

What does poor service look like? Because you are also a customer, you know the specifics. Here are the top 10 for review:

1. Lack of manners.
2. Rude, discourteous behavior.
3. Long waits on the phone.
4. Long waits in line.
5. Lack of knowledge of the product or policy.
6. Lack of follow-through.
7. Not resolving a complaint.
8. Unresponsive technology or not knowing how to use it.
9. Inability to reach a real person.
10. Unfulfilled promises, lies, and other deceptions.

When you think about it, all of these are inexcusable in a business environment. If you delivered that type of service to yourself as a customer, how would you feel? Would you be disappointed, frustrated, confused, angry, upset, inconvenienced, irritated, or even outraged? Would you complain? Would you demand better treatment? Sure you would. As a customer service person, do you want to do that to a customer? Of course not!

What are some examples of awful service? You probably have a few of your own to tell. Take a look at a few of our personal experiences:

▶ After we were seated at a restaurant, the waitress came over, put her hand on her hip, and said, "Hurry up and order. I am off in five minutes."

▶ We checked in late to a hotel where we were doing a seminar. We asked the hotel clerk about the box of materials we sent. He replied, "I don't know where they are, mister. No one tells us anything on the night shift."

▶ An airline had multiple delays for our flight. When we asked the flight agent what was going on she replied, "I don't know. Nobody is telling us anything. Please be patient." The flight was delayed seven hours, and no real apology or compensation was given.

▶ We called a computer manufacturer about a glitch in our system. We were bounced around to five people, if not five countries, and no answer was given. Multiple repair tickets were written, but no action fixed the problem. Of course, they never did call back. We had to call and wait forever on the line before we got to a live customer service representative.

▶ We needed to get a car repaired. The bill exceeded the estimate significantly. The service advisor accused us of trying to get free service when we questioned the bill. We asked to talk to the general manager; he wasn't in. We never got a call back. We had to call him. The general manager said he checked it out, and that the service advisor had been there 20 years and was one of his most reliable employees, and we would get no adjustment.

These examples are inexcusable, yet they happen every day. Don't let this be you. Customers won't settle for this. They will take their money and go elsewhere.

Loyal customers are like golden eggs, and companies who cater to them win. Those who don't, lose. Research from TARP, the Strategic Planning Institute, Bain, the U.S. Office of Consumer Affairs, and ACSI all demonstrate that leading service companies outperform all others. Companies that internalize this see dramatic gains in customer loyalty and sales growth. Companies that lag behind in their service delivery, struggle in their drive to succeed. You would think that wouldn't be the case, but it happens very frequently. Large corporations often say one thing and do another, focusing more on the metrics of expense control, or upgrading services through new and advanced technology. The supermarket industry, for example, uses self-checkout despite the fact that recent research shows that most customers find self-checkout to be a nuisance. Many companies use automated phone systems despite the fact that they are an affront to personal service. What customer hasn't been delayed and annoyed by an automated phone system that gives endless options? In this age of instant texts and social media buzz, these archaic tools disregard customer service as a whole.

When you really analyze the market, it is clear that it isn't that hard to be the best in service in the industry. Why? Because so many companies are bad at it. This is an opportune time for enterprising companies and individuals to seize the concept of excellent customer service and make it a standard for their business practices.

So, what is Superstar customer service? It's what few achieve. It's the business equivalent to the superstars of sports and entertainment. What company wouldn't want their employees to be thought of with the notoriety of such great performers as Michael Jordan, Lebron James, Brad Pitt, Tina Turner, Roger Federer, the Stones, or Lady Gaga? Imagine that for yourself. Why not you? Believe it could happen. These thoughts are the beginning of you becoming a genuine customer service Superstar.

Believe it about you! Superstars break through and excel where others fall short. Superstars deliver exceptional personal care no matter what the industry. Superstars are consistent and passionate about helping, and they go to extraordinary levels to deliver. This is the essence of this book. Stay tuned to find out how to reach Superstar status.

> *Merely satisfying customers will not be enough to earn their loyalty. Instead, they must experience exceptional service worthy of their repeat business and referral. Understand the factors that drive this customer revolution.*
>
> —Rick Tate

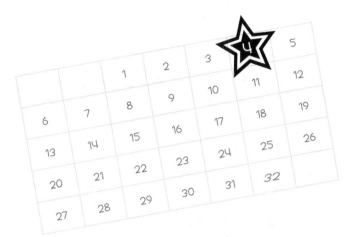

# What Does It Mean to Manage Myself?
## *The Power of Positivity*

Your attitude is your greatest resource. It defines everything from your personal state of being to your interactions with others, and plays a key role in your professional success. Motivator Zig Ziglar said, "It's your attitude, not your aptitude, that determines your altitude." According to a behavioral study cited by Bob Conklin, this could not be more true. The study found that 93 percent of the success of an individual is due to his or her attitude.[1] Only 7 percent of his or her success is due to job knowledge, communication skills, and technical expertise. People with a positive attitude learn what they need to know and get results. Because of this, your attitude is instrumental in managing yourself and achieving your personal and professional goals. There are three fundamental elements for proper self-management, each of which is rooted in a positive attitude:

1. Learn all you can!

2. Expect the best of yourself and others!

3. Believe you cannot fail!

## Learn All You Can!

We believe if you increase your learning, you will increase your earning. Some companies build excellent learning opportunities into the job.

For example, Disney Corporation theme parks offer more training to young employees than most veteran managers or salespeople will ever get. However, many times employees are left with very few opportunities to learn something new or build a new skill. No matter the circumstance, taking learning and advancement into your control will empower you to live up to your full potential. For Superstars, learning is a do-it-yourself project. Lifelong learning will become habit, and finding learning opportunities will become second nature.

So what you can do? Learning resources can be found anywhere from the bookstore to YouTube. First, read this book diligently and apply the exercises. Then, read other books that relate to your job. Go online and search for related material. Most of it is free. Listen to CDs and watch DVDs. If you can't figure out where to start, visit our blog (*www.wcwpartnersblog.com*) and you'll find a wealth of written and video material that can help anyone increase effectiveness. Above all, be a student of game; be responsible for your own learning, knowledge, and skill. Leaders in every field do this and excel. Self-manage your success; it's in your hands.

## Expect the Best of Yourself and Others!

Imagine the results if every time you went fishing you said the following:

▶ "I won't catch anything, as usual."

▶ "I hate sitting in the boat."

▶ "The lakes are too crowded."

▶ "My buddy's a clod and will screw everything up."

▶ "This is going to be boring."

Would you enjoy fishing? Would you purchase new tackle or try new spots to improve your catch? No way! You probably wouldn't even go. Your negative attitude already predicted the potential outcome. You "gotta wanna," or you won't become a Superstar.

In the 1984 Olympics, Mary Lou Retton was down to her last jump in the vault. She was in second place, behind a Romanian gymnast. Mary Lou needed a 9.95 to tie for the gold medal and a perfect 10.0 to win. What do you think her attitude was? Was her inner monologue *"I can't do it. My coach is a jerk. I'm nervous and scared. Oh no, millions of people are watching. I hope I don't trip"*?

Denis Waitley, motivator and behavioral psychologist, talked to Mary Lou after the event. Remember: As an Olympic athlete, she had invested years in preparation, training, and competition. She told herself she had to run hard, extend, tuck, and plant. She had done it before and believed she'd do it again. Mary Lou said that she told herself, "I need a 10. Get a 10. This one is for you, Mom and Dad." Then boom—she acted and took off. She got a 10. She didn't go for a tie; she went for and won the gold. Then she did it again on another jump. She expected the best and achieved the best she could, because she believed in herself and told herself she could do it.

## Believe You Cannot Fail!

Your mind will do what you program it to do. Are you setting yourself up for service failure or success? A department store was having problems with theft. As a way to combat the problem, the store played a subliminal message with the background music. The message said, "Don't steal; shoplifters will be prosecuted." Shoplifting went up 25 percent. The negative message actually encouraged people to steal. So the store changed the message to say, "Be nice and honest. Pay at the cashier." The result? Shoplifting went down.

What messages do you give yourself or your coworkers? Do you always criticize what's happening or complain about customers? Problems with coworkers, complaints, lost customers, and even sickness will set you up for failure. Your thoughts over time will rule your actions. Why not do it differently?

When people learn to do things one way consistently, they quickly become habits. Then, no matter how hard they try to change, things stay the same because they become ingrained in their nature. They can't see themselves differently. Promises aren't kept, New Year's resolutions are broken, diets aren't followed, relationships fail, and bills aren't paid. It seems that it is nearly impossible to change or get ahead in life. The good news is people can change. The only way to get rid of old habits is to build new ones.

Before you can get into a new habit, it is important to take a step back and identify what you are currently doing. Look at the repercussions and ask yourself why you are doing it and what changes you would like to make. Then, look at yourself differently. Don't get stuck in your old ways; set goals to make changes happen and then work toward them.

David Stevens believed he couldn't fail. One day, he went to the annual Minnesota Twins tryout camp. The Twins' officials were flabbergasted; they couldn't understand why David was trying out. You see, David had no legs. The Twins' managers talked to David to find out who he was and learned he was a champion wrestler, hit .500 on his high school baseball team, and played middle guard in football. The officials asked him, "Why are you trying out? You aren't going to make the team." David responded that he didn't have to be at work until 2 p.m., so why not try out? He had no limits or boundaries.

How many of us never try? We'd think of failing, or how we are different, or what other people would say. It is time to stop believing it. Like a tiny acorn that has the pattern of a mighty oak tree in it, you have talent, strengths, and potential! Expect the best in all that you do, have pride, believe in success, and don't dwell on the possibility of failure. Each mistake is an opportunity to learn and improve. You have to work at it; this kind of approach doesn't come easy or free. However, through using the concepts we are outlining, it is possible.

To maximize your potential through self-management, you must step outside yourself, and look at where you are and where you want to go. What are your strengths? What are your weaknesses? What are you learning from customers? Co-workers? Your boss? What do you need to learn to be better at what you do? Once you've asked yourself these questions, you are on the road to successful, dynamic results. The first step to changing where you are requires knowing where you are starting.

Consider the famous quote by famed Green Bay Packers coach Vince Lombardi: "You'll never be perfect. Aim for perfection and you'll achieve excellence." With a foundation of a positive attitude and the elements we have discussed, taking care of customers and living life are a lot easier and more enjoyable. Complete the following exercise to summarize your commitment to becoming a customer service Superstar.

| Superstar Application: YOU:<br>A Customer Service Superstar! | |
| --- | --- |
| I am motivated by… | What I like most about my job is… |
| My strengths are... | My customers like me because... |
| I will improve... | I am a customer service Superstar because... |

*Every contact we have with a customer influences whether or not they'll come back. We have to be great every time or we'll lose them.*

—Kevin Stirtz

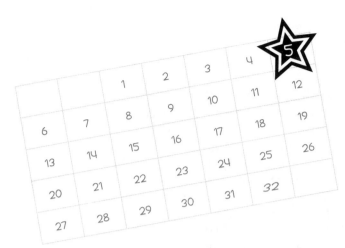

## To What Standards Should I Try to Rise?

Answer these questions:

I►  Do you believe you have it in you?

I►  Do you believe you can do it?

I►  Do you think you have what it takes?

Are you wondering what "it" is? Do your answers depend on it? If you answered yes to either of these two questions, answer this one: *Why? Why do your answers depend on what "it" is and not on you?* Anytime you're relying on something other than yourself to define your abilities or to answer what's asked of you, it's a surefire sign that you're not tapping into your truest capability and potential.

What if you answered these questions in one of these three ways?

1. *I believe I have tremendous talent and desire within me!*

2. *I believe I can do anything I set my mind to!*

3. *I believe I will do whatever it takes to deliver Superstar customer service!*

Do you believe in your own capability? If so, how are you maximizing your potential? These are deep questions, which require careful analysis and intentional action. If you hope to utilize the unlimited potential that's buried in your beliefs, then you must release the reserve of capability that's at your core. If you don't believe in it, you are suffocating your potential success.

In the world of customer service, it's easy to do just enough to get by. A routine starts, every day is the same, and a certain weariness of the "same old, same old" can set in. The mentality of "There will always be another customer, so why make your interaction with this one any more than ordinary?" is to be expected, right? Wrong! Today competition is worldwide. Everyone competes with everyone. Winning companies need to constantly change to improve products, prices, quality, innovation, and service. Because of the changing landscape of business today, employees must think more about their impact. Those who choose, rise above everyone else to deliver excellent service, excel.

## Your Personal Standards

Have you ever felt a high? If you ask people how they feel when they have a high, they'll usually say good, confident, or problem free. You can feel this way and get a natural high by achieving your life desires and goals.

Arnold Lemerand knows what it is to get a high. One day, he took his daily walk. As he passed by a construction site, he heard some children frantically screaming. He hurried to their location, where he spotted a young boy with his head pinned under a sewage pipe. If he didn't act quickly, the pipe would suffocate the boy in the sand. What could he do? Without a second thought, he did the only thing possible: He lifted the 1,600-pound pipe and the boy was freed. Later in an interview with the UPI, Arnold explained that he had a heart attack recently and the doctor told him not to lift heavy items. The pipe was so heavy that his two teenage sons tried to lift the pipe and couldn't. So how did he manage to lift the pipe? He acted in an emergency, summoned his body's reserve potential, and lifted the pipe. He felt a high and was able to do remarkable things![1] Everyone can tap these reserves and fulfill their full potential; you just need to work at it.

## The Problem

Often our own thinking locks us into a prison with no escape. So many people who deliver customer service in their jobs are stuck like this and don't know that their minds are their keys to freedom.

## The Possibility

The brain contains substances that make it possible to completely change your state of mind. The medical field has identified five key natural hormones in the brain: encephalin, endorphin, beta-endorphin, dynorphin, and adrenaline. Doctors call these "keys" pain relievers. In other words, if people are sad, frustrated, dejected, or even physically hurt, access to these hormones can overcome the pain and create more positive responses.

In one study, a group of people received shots of these hormones. A second group was injected with a placebo. Both groups showed significant gains in belief, confidence, and faith in themselves. The researchers concluded that the simple act of fascination over frustration, belief over doubt, and confidence over fear, causes the individual to embody that feeling, no matter if he or she received the placebo or the real thing. In other words, you have the potential to control your own outcome. If you're feeling negative, act positively and soon your brain will start to align with your actions. Sometimes you need to "fake it 'til you make it," and you will make it.

The power of this possibility became a case study in Norman Cousins, editor of the *Saturday Review.* In 1964, he contracted a rare disease. His doctor predicted he'd die soon. Cousins went ahead and checked himself out of the hospital, because it was only creating negative emotions. He rented a room somewhere else and every day watched Marx Brothers and Candid Camera movies, which made him laugh. The positive emotions of joy and laughter accessed his natural pain relieving hormones and healed him. Your brain has limitless potential to control your outcomes, but to do so you need to believe you can.

## The Present

What are you high on? What is your state of mind or attitude? Psychologist William James wrote, "The greatest discovery of our generation is that people can alter the outer aspects of their lives by changing the inner attitudes of their minds."[2] How can you do this to raise your personal standards and achieve stardom while delivering customer service in your job?

Here are four helpful strategies to get you started:

1. **Affirm yourself.** In other words, intentionally choose to believe positive things about yourself. After you've thought of them, write them down and reflect on them regularly.

2. **Learn from mistakes, but don't linger on them.** When you fail or fall short, reflect on your shortcomings only long enough to learn from them. Then move on. After a mistake, the majority of your mental work should be devoted to picking out the positive, building on it, and applying it again and again.

3. **Maintain perspective. Belief builds upon belief.** It takes hundreds of minor movements to make it up a mountain, in the same way that it takes several small steps to achieve success. So, be patient with yourself as you attempt to alter your attitude. It's all about perspective; the way you looked at something yesterday might not be worlds away from your approach today, but as long as you have a different angle, you're making progress.

4. **Keep learning.** If we aren't learning and growing, we are decaying and dying. As you increase your learning in life, you increase your earning. Your efforts with this book are a great place to start. Keep at it and apply the information.

Career success is simple: Believe that you can achieve greatness and you will be able to. You have been given the opportunity to control how you see the world and how you do your job. In that, you have all of the tools that you need to succeed. By tapping these resources and getting yourself into the right frame of mind you will be well on your way to becoming a customer service Superstar.

> *Friendly makes sales—and friendly*
> *generates repeat business.*
>
> —Jeffrey Gitomer

## The Difference Between Good Service and Superstar Service

The difference between good customer service and abysmal customer service is usually pretty clear. It can be the difference between walking into a store and being completely ignored, and walking in and being greeted politely. What isn't as clear is what differentiates good customer service from Superstar customer service. To better understand Superstar customer service, it is best to look at what defines a customer.

### The Definition of a Customer

A customer is someone who receives and benefits from something you are offering. These benefits may come in the form of a product, service, or even just information, whether there is an exchange of money or not.

Customers can be internal or external, low on the totem pole or high on the ladder, your peer or your partner, and so forth. Narrowing your definition of "customers" only limits your ability to satisfy the individual and generate success for both them and yourself. Frequently, successful individuals and companies define "service" too narrowly, therefore limiting their opportunity for more success. For example, one widely known company prides itself on having the lowest prices for its customers, but it also has the worst customer service in its industry. Though it is a successful company, its narrow definition of how it helps customers seriously erodes the potential success it will be able to achieve. Exceeding customers' expectations is important to good leaders in any industry. By satisfying customers, they are able to secure their business with them in the present *and* in the future.

Superstar focus on customer service means more than just knowing your product or service well; it means interacting with your customer on a basic human level. Doctors are trained for eight years in their profession including their education and internship. Some do even more. Have you ever had a doctor who was technically excellent but had a horrible bedside manner? Their poor bedside manner will invariably cost them patients that they could have helped. Callous people skills and lack of empathy actually wears heavily on doctors' ability to help their patients heal, so even though they have the clinical training and skills, they may not be as effective.

Regardless of your industry, experience, or background, think about *your customers* and what they need or want from you technically and personally to have a Superstar customer experience. Make a list of everyone who currently benefits from what you have to offer. These are your first priorities, because they are immediate opportunities. Afterward, consider those who *could* benefit from what you have to offer or have a special need that you believe you *could* fulfill.

A Superstar is the cab driver who treats his cab like a limo; it's sparkling clean with updated reading material. He offers refreshments to all who ride. He gets their name and gives them a business card. He engages each person and gets to know him or her. His goal? For you to ride in his cab anytime you are in his city and to tell others about him.

A Superstar is the flight attendant who uses your name as she delivers service to you with a sense of humor and joy. She appropriately engages you and serves you. She uses good manners while she serves the person next to you and reaches across your seating area. She gives you a thank-you card for riding the airline with her business card. She also gives you a survey to rate her service.

A Superstar is the mechanic who "owns" your automobile while he does maintenance. He gives you a ride to and from the shop, or arranges one for you. He treats you like royalty whether you have a beater or a Lexus. He calls and keeps you updated, and tries to save you money on needed repairs.

A Superstar is the waiter who makes eye contact when he talks to you with charm and friendliness. He is candid about what was good or not as good, knows his menu and wines, and is promptly attentive and appreciative. He remembers you from previous dinners and his banter adds a fun atmosphere to dining out.

## Superstar Customer Service

So, why do you want to deliver Superstar customer service? What are your reasons?

▶ Make more money?

▶ Achieve your goals?

▶ Surpass your company goals?

▶ Obtain more job satisfaction?

▶ Gain more recognition?

▶ Advance your career?

We identified the competencies of Customer Service Superstars in Day 2. In Day 7 and Day 8, we will define them in detail and give you the opportunity to assess your skills compared to those competencies and do action planning for success.

Throughout your journey to becoming a Superstar customer service representative, keep in mind the three characteristics that set Superstars apart:

1. **Personal empowerment.** If you look at your role simply as being a rodent running the rat race, you won't find satisfaction and motivation long-term. You will get burnt out and frustrated well before your time. But, if you feel as though you are the one in control, you are much more likely to *take* control over what you can. This includes your relationship with your customers, whoever you identify them to be. To be personally empowered means you do your job, and take full responsibility and accountability for your results.

2. **Personal brand.** At every business, on every team, and in every industry, your personal brand matters. Your personal brand is how you differentiate yourself from others; it is how you highlight your assets and define what you do in the workplace. Your personal brand is of supreme importance when it comes to your success. For this reason, if you're constantly treating everyone and anyone like a customer, you will be that much more aware and intentional about how you listen to, treat, and help others. Consequently, they will be that much more likely to remember and respect you, and willing to receive what you have to offer.

3. **Personal service.** Superstars positively engage their customers. Each customer is like a close friend or family member. Rae, a friend of ours, had an uncommon but learned ability to relate to anyone. Though she passed away a few years ago after a long bout with cancer, if she was alive and met you now, within five minutes you would swear she was your best friend. She knew how to make every person feel comfortable and cared about. Superstars learn the people skills, manners, and the ability to communicate and put themselves in the customers' shoes. They identify with their customers and earn their trust honestly.

Having good customer service is essential to having a successful business. Having Superstar customer service will not only differentiate you from the rest, it will bring your business and your success to the next level.

*When people talk about successful retailers
and those that are not so successful, the
customer determines at the end of the day
who is successful and for what reason.*

—Jerry Harvey

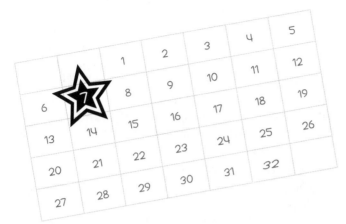

# How Do I Currently Stack Up?

## The Changing Reality in the Customer Service World

Change in business is occurring faster than ever. For the last 20 years or more, businesses have been installing and adapting to new technology and increasingly reaping the benefits of advancements in information technology. It has the potential to help businesses reach more customers, streamline operations, reduce costs, improve efficiency, maximize profit, minimize waste, and provide better service to customers. More and more, today's consumers are increasingly comfortable and empowered by the use of the powerful technological tools at their fingertips 24 hours a day. It's estimated that there will be 2.5 billion smartphones on the planet by 2020.[1] Think about the implications and how they relate to how business is done.

The days when you simply needed to know product information to provide customer service are gone. Consumers already know their options. They have done or are doing their own research on the products they're interested in, and have immediate access to pricing and, perhaps more importantly, other customer's experiences and feedback. This goes right down to the quality of service provided by each employee. They are not impressed with your product knowledge, and they may very well know as much about the product as you do. They are hyper-aware of what you promise and will blow the whistle on you immediately if you don't deliver on your promises. They will communicate with your company and millions of social media users on the spot if they are less than delighted with your customer service.

These changing realities also dictate changing requirements in the world of customer service. A great deal of the power in the relationship has shifted to the consumer. It has always been best to be customer-centered. Now it is absolutely essential. You must have the skill and the will to connect with your customers, genuinely and effectively. You need to be able to "sell without selling," while still being proficient at listening to understand and seamlessly plugging into their problems or needs. It's important that you anticipate without getting ahead of them, and join to meet their needs and fill in with your experience and deeper understanding. Finally, you must be helpful and concerned without being overbearing.

Customer service has increasingly become a different animal than it was a few years ago. If you're really going to stand out based on your service, you're going to have to be great. The following is a self-assessment designed to give you a "read" on your competencies (current skill and behavior) as a customer service provider. Once you've taken the assessment you'll find guidance on how to score and interpret your assessment in Day 8. Finally, you'll receive guidance on steps you might take to further develop your capabilities in this area.

## Superstar Customer Service Assessment

**Introduction:** The purpose of this assessment is to give you an opportunity to review your customer service skill level based on the core competencies for Superstar customer service. What is needed here is your total honesty. Each of the statements is presented in the context of meeting customer service responsibilities, whether in a retail setting or a highly tech setting. Use the scale and write the number of your response in the space provided to the left of each item to indicate *how likely you are* to **use each of these Customer Service Behaviors.**

Response Scale

| 6 | 5 | 4 | 3 | 2 | 1 |
|---|---|---|---|---|---|
| This is definitely like you. | This is like you. | This is somewhat like you. | This is somewhat unlike you. | This is unlike you. | This is definitely unlike you. |

| | Select a number from the scale to indicate how likely you are to: |
|---|---|
| | 1. Get ready to do your job, knowing that there will be challenges ahead. |
| | 2. Remain focused on your professional role when you're challenged by difficult situations. |
| | 3. Make sure your work is "up to standards" before moving on to the next customer or task. |
| Total Competency: | |
| | 4. Greet the customer warmly. |
| | 5. Ask, "How may I help you?" |
| | 6. Patiently work through the customer's problems, even if they're expressed inappropriately. |
| Total Competency: | |
| | 7. Manage your time to be productive working with your customers to meet their needs. |
| | 8. Begin your day with a well-organized plan, focused on the most important tasks to complete. |
| | 9. Stay focused on your priorities rather than getting swept away with random "to-do's." |
| Total Competency: | |
| | 10. Consistently maintain a focus on producing error-free" results. |
| | 11. Strive to be productive 100 percent of the time on the job—no slacking off. |
| | 12. Manage your efforts in order to maintain a consistent and high level of productivity |
| Total Competency: | |

| | |
|---|---|
| | 13. Know what you need to accomplish in order to do your job. |
| | 14. Maintain consistent effort so your time on the job is always directed productively. |
| | 15. Set up goals, plans, and measures to guide your efforts and measure your outcomes. |
| Total Competency: | |
| | 16. Listen actively to ensure that you understand your customer's needs, fully and completely. |
| | 17. Manage your biases and judgments to gain a clean perspective on your customer's needs. |
| | 18. Avoid getting sidetracked by personal judgment of customer motives or character. |
| Total Competency: | |
| | 19. Communicate in a clear, understandable, and respectful manner. |
| | 20. Translate complex information into messages that are understandable for each customer. |
| | 21. Communicate in an empathetic manner, especially when expressing "bad news." |
| Total Competency: | |
| | 22. Quickly get to "the heart of the matter" when diagnosing customer problems. |
| | 23. Separate irrelevant information from information central to diagnosis and resolution. |
| | 24. Carefully monitor your impact on your customer to maintain an open environment. |
| Total Competency: | |

| | |
|---|---|
| | 25. See the difference between "symptoms" of complex problems and the root causes. |
| | 26. See obstacles that must be removed to achieve the customer's desired outcomes. |
| | 27. Avoid "shooting in the dark" on solutions that may cause additional problems. |
| Total Competency: | |
| | 28. Offer appropriate reality-based information to help customers decide to invest in available solutions or not, based on their criteria. |
| | 29. Avoid getting ahead of the customer and generating anxiety or frustration when they must decide. |
| | 30. Follow the customer's wishes even when there is another choice you would prefer. |
| Total Competency: | |
| | 31. Use objective measures the customer can follow to distinguish valid from flawed diagnosis. |
| | 32. Gently steer the customer from flawed assumptions about the cause of their problems. |
| | 33. Patiently explain, using facts and reasoning, when the solution isn't what the customer prefers. |
| Total Competency: | |
| | 34. Actively avoid customers by moving away from them when you're busy or stressed. |
| | 35. Give minimal engagement—just enough to get by when you're tired or overwhelmed. |
| | 36. Withhold eye contact or divert your attention to something other than the customer when you are already busy. |
| Total Competency: | |

| | |
|---|---|
| | 37. Respond defensively when a customer gets angry or rude. |
| | 38. React aggressively when customers blame you or your company for their problems. |
| | 39. Let customers know "they can't treat you that way" when they shout or curse. |
| Total Competency: | |
| | 40. Tell customers "what they did wrong" when you can see that the problem is their "own fault." |
| | 41. Show your disgust when it's clear that they're lying or don't know what they're talking about. |
| | 42. Give customers a look that says, "I'm not playing that game" when they're acting mean or unprofessional. |
| Total Competency: | |

Now that you've rated yourself on each of the items in the self-assessment, and you've totaled your scores for each of the 14 competency areas, you can read the competency descriptions for Superstar customer service on the next pages. These short descriptions will provide you with a clear picture of the skill and competency set we'll be discussing in the remainder of this book. It will also prepare you to complete your scoring, interpretation, and action planning in Day 8.

> *If you do build a great experience, customers tell each other about that. Word of mouth is very powerful.*
> —Jeff Bezos, CEO, Amazon.com

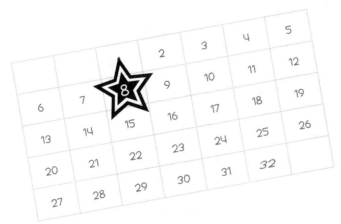

# What Do I Need to Improve and Why?
*Interpretation and Action Planning*

In Day 7, you took the opportunity to compare your current customer service practices, skills, and behaviors to those presented in our Superstar customer service model. You also had a chance to familiarize yourself with the specific skills and behaviors that comprise each of the 14 competencies and to identify any tendencies you have to use service behaviors that undermine your effectiveness. In this chapter, you'll take the next steps to plug your total numbers into the scoring and interpretation guides, and narrow your focus to the areas that will most help you to develop Superstar customer service skills. First is the scoring sheet, followed by the interpretation key and interpretation guide. Once you've completed your interpretation, you will be ready to plan specific action steps for your improvement and ongoing development.

## SuperSTAR Customer Service Assessment Scoring Sheet

**Instructions:** Transfer your total scores from each section of the Superstar Customer Service Assessment Sheet to the appropriate spaces on this scoring sheet.

| Items | Measures | Score | |
|-------|----------|-------|--|
| 1–3 | Managing Myself (Total Competency 1) | | |
| 4–6 | Manage Customer Relationships (Total Competency 2) | | |
| 7–9 | Manage My Time (Total Competency 3) | | |
| 10–12 | Achieve Results (Total Competency 4) | | |
| 13–15 | Personal Productivity (Total Competency 5) | | |
| 16–18 | Listening (Total Competency 6) | | |
| 19–21 | Communicate Clearly (Total Competency 7) | | |
| 22–24 | Gather Useful Information (Total Competency 8) | | |
| 25–37 | Solve Problems (Total Competency 9) | | |
| 28–30 | Make Decisions (Total Competency 10) | | |
| 31–33 | Think Clearly (Total Competency 11) | | |
| 34–36 | Avoidant Behavior (Total Competency 12) See page 49. | | |
| 37–39 | Hostile Behavior (Total Competency 13) See page 49. | | |
| 40–42 | Judgmental Behavior (Total Competency 14) See page 49. | | |

**Note:** The scores for the last nine items in the survey (34–42) represent negative behaviors. The scores for those items should be reversed before totaling the scores:

| Original Score | Becomes This Score |
|:---:|:---:|
| 6 | 1 |
| 5 | 2 |
| 4 | 3 |
| 3 | 4 |
| 2 | 5 |
| 1 | 6 |

A score of 6 is changed to a 1, a 5 becomes a 4 becomes a 3, a 3 becomes a 4, a 5 becomes a 2, and a 1 becomes a 6.

## Interpretation Key

Use the scale for each leadership dimension to place your score within the interpretation key. Place a check mark into the range where your score falls.

| Service Dimension | Score | ✓ |
|---|:---:|---|
| Managing Myself (Items numbered 1–3) | **15–18** | ☐ Superstar service strength |
| | **11–14** | ☐ Strong competence |
| | **7–10** | ☐ Development recommended |
| | **3–6** | ☐ Area that needs immediate work |
| Manage Customer Relationships (Items numbered 4–6) | **15–18** | ☐ Superstar service strength |
| | **11–14** | ☐ Strong competence |
| | **7–10** | ☐ Development recommended |
| | **3–6** | ☐ Area that needs immediate work |

| Service Dimension | Score | ✓ |
|---|---|---|
| Manage My Time (Items numbered 7–9) | 15–18 | ☐ Superstar service strength |
| | 11–14 | ☐ Strong competence |
| | 7–10 | ☐ Development recommended |
| | 3–6 | ☐ Area that needs immediate work |
| Achieve Results (Items numbered 10–12) | 15–18 | ☐ Superstar service strength |
| | 11–14 | ☐ Strong competence |
| | 7–10 | ☐ Development recommended |
| | 3–6 | ☐ Area that needs immediate work |
| Personal Productivity (Items numbered 13–15) | 15–18 | ☐ Superstar service strength |
| | 11–14 | ☐ Strong competence |
| | 7–10 | ☐ Development recommended |
| | 3–6 | ☐ Area that needs immediate work |
| Listening (Items numbered 16–18) | 15–18 | ☐ Superstar service strength |
| | 11–14 | ☐ Strong competence |
| | 7–10 | ☐ Development recommended |
| | 3–6 | ☐ Area that needs immediate work |

| Service Dimension | Score | ✓ |
|---|---|---|
| Communicate Clearly (Items numbered 19–21) | 15–18 | ☐ Superstar service strength |
| | 11–14 | ☐ Strong competence |
| | 7–10 | ☐ Development recommended |
| | 3–6 | ☐ Area that needs immediate work |
| Gather Useful Information (Items numbered 22–24) | 15–18 | ☐ Superstar service strength |
| | 11–14 | ☐ Strong competence |
| | 7–10 | ☐ Development recommended |
| | 3–6 | ☐ Area that needs immediate work |
| Solve Problems (Items numbered 25–27) | 15–18 | ☐ Superstar service strength |
| | 11–14 | ☐ Strong competence |
| | 7–10 | ☐ Development recommended |
| | 3–6 | ☐ Area that needs immediate work |
| Make Decisions (Items numbered 28–30) | 15–18 | ☐ Superstar service strength |
| | 11–14 | ☐ Strong competence |
| | 7–10 | ☐ Development recommended |
| | 3–6 | ☐ Area that needs immediate work |

| Service Dimension | Score | ✓ |
|---|---|---|
| Think Clearly (Items numbered 31–33) | 15–18 | ☐ Superstar service strength |
| | 11–14 | ☐ Strong competence |
| | 7–10 | ☐ Development recommended |
| | 3–6 | ☐ Area that needs immediate work |
| Avoidant Behavior (Items numbered 34–36) | 15–18 | ☐ Superstar service strength |
| | 11–14 | ☐ Strong competence |
| | 7–10 | ☐ Development recommended |
| | 3–6 | ☐ Area that needs immediate work |
| Hostile Behavior (Items numbered 37–39) | 15–18 | ☐ Superstar service strength |
| | 11–14 | ☐ Strong competence |
| | 7–10 | ☐ Development recommended |
| | 3–6 | ☐ Area that needs immediate work |
| Judgmental Behavior (Items numbered 40–42) | 15–18 | ☐ Superstar service strength |
| | 11–14 | ☐ Strong competence |
| | 7–10 | ☐ Development recommended |
| | 3–6 | ☐ Area that needs immediate work |

**Note:** The last three rows (Items numbered 34–42) are comprised of items that have a negative impact on service relationships and outcomes. Your scores for these items should have been reversed prior to totaling them. Your total should then lead you to the proper service description category.

## Interpretation Guide

Compare your score for this section to the score descriptions that follow, and use the "Suggestions for Action" to guide you in pursuing development in this area.

| Score | Suggestions for Action |
|---|---|
| **Superstar Service Strength** | Your scores indicate that you are using these *critical* customer service skills and behaviors *routinely*. Remember that we are constantly changing, as is the world around us. Never remain static. It's frequently said that if you aren't growing, you're going backward. Read the related pages for a review of your current strengths. Look for ideas and inspiration to make the area of strength even more powerful for you as a service Superstar. |
| **Strong Competence** | The skills contained in this section are familiar to you and are a primary source of your current effectiveness. Study this area and complete the daily application to add additional depth and richness your current customer service strengths. After you've reviewed the entire section and completed the application, go back to any areas where you rated yourself a "3" or below, and develop additional plans to deepen your knowledge further apply these skills. Remember: Knowing is important. But, unless you regularly *do* the service actions contained here, they are not impacting your customers. |

| Score | Suggestions for Action |
|---|---|
| **Development Recommended** | If your total score for this area is in the "development recommended" range, there is significant opportunity for you to learn and improve your customer service impact. Re-read this section and commit to the service actions for practice and review over a three-to-six-month period of time. Focus on increasing your use of the items where you rated your use higher (e.g., 3–5). In other words, build on your relative strengths. Identify the ones where you scored yourself lowest and commit to doing those service actions frequently over an extended time (e.g., three to six months). Remember: The value of these actions is not up for debate. They have already been proven. Your challenge is to practice these and make them part of your regular customer service repertoire. |
| **Area That Needs Immediate Work** | If your score places you in the "needs immediate work" range for this section you have significant opportunity to grow as a service provider. Whether you are new and less experienced in your role, or simply haven't "bought" these concepts as important to your success, you have much to gain by learning about and applying these concepts and skills fully. Your attention to developing here may be the difference between your success and failure. |

When reviewing your scores within each service dimension, identify any behaviors where your rating was a 1 or 2. Pay particular attention to these areas for development. Otherwise, they may undermine your current effectiveness and future potential. Also remember that any use of the behaviors that are labeled Avoidant, Hostile, and/or Judgmental have an "outsized" negative impact on your customer relationship. In other words, they have a multiplied negative impact that is very difficult to recover from. These behaviors have no place in a customer service role. You'll need to recognize and change these common behaviors quickly.

| Action Planning |
|---|
| 1. A. List competency areas that are clearly growth opportunities for you. |
| B. Choose two or three that would give you the biggest "bang for the buck." |

| Areas of Growth Opportunities for Me Right Now | Areas in Which Immediate Improvement Would Help Me the Most Right Now |
|---|---|
| | |

2. What's in it for you to grow in these areas?

| Action Planning (continued) |
|---|
| 3. What have you tried before? What worked? |
| 4. What resources are available to support you in these developmental opportunities? |
| 5. What are your intended first steps? |

| Action Planning (continued) |
|---|
| 6. Who needs to know about this? |
| 7. How will you enlist others to help you? |

*Unless you have 100% customer*
*satisfaction...you must improve.*

—Horst Schulz

# It All Begins With a Problem

One of the beautiful things about customer service is that you get the opportunity to directly help customers. Customers are people. They are fellow companies and individual consumers—men and women, young and old—who buy your product. Even when your customer is a company, people are still the ones who make the purchases. The key consideration for a customer service representative is the customer's satisfaction with his or her experience with your company. The events and interactions that occur during and after the purchase between the customer service person or persons and the customer will dictate the degree of their satisfaction.

Ideally, every product does what it says it will do. In other words, the quality of the product meets every expectation. Apple's iPad is expected to turn on and off and have superb graphics. A restaurant's food is expected to taste great. A car is expected to operate flawlessly. A grocery store's produce must be fresh and edible. Clothes should fit nicely, look great after being cleaned, and wear well. Customers purchasing these things are pleased when their purchases perform as they expected. Ideally, the service delivery for each of these products goes well, too. The customer service delivered by employees should be courteous, helpful, knowledge-able, and timely. They might also try to add an extra touch to make the experience a more positive and memorable event.

It almost always begins with a problem. How often does everything work ideally? Let's say eight out of the 10 times you buy apples they are good, whereas the other two times they are rotten. Would you accept rotten apples 20 percent of the time? Let's say you travel often. An airline boasts that it is safe 95 percent of the time. Now, this is much better than the grocer's performance, but would you fly on an airline with a 5 percent crash rate? Your answer is likely "absolutely not!" In each of these situations, incident rates need to be significantly lower to get your business. Shouldn't we expect that all the apples we buy are edible? If they aren't, what will you or other customers do? You'll probably begin shopping elsewhere. Airlines can't afford any mistakes or people die. Air travel has to be safe, without exception, or it doesn't have an industry. These two examples are about the product. In the manufacturing industry today, they aim for zero defects. This means less than one defect per million parts produced, a number that few companies have achieved. The new standard is less than one defect per billion parts produced. We know that all products deteriorate with time. Clothes, batteries, computers, engine parts, washing machines, and sporting equipment all wear out. Food, gasoline, and cleaning products are either consumed or expire. We expect this because it's the natural order of things. However, the higher the quality of the product, the longer it is likely to perform well. Customers want the longest-lasting products that they can find for a given price range. What do we do when things break down or have problems sooner than we expect? We either complain or we shop elsewhere next time. Sometimes we do both.

With every product there is service delivery. Do we have zero defects in the service delivery of the product? Would you accept a waitress who swears at you or leaves you waiting an extraordinary amount of time before asking for your order? Let's assume that your car needs a tune-up. You make an appointment at the auto dealer for the necessary maintenance. You have to take off work to bring your car in and they say, "Sorry, you don't have an appointment today." Would you accept that? Or let's say you're shopping online for some jewelry. Would you use a site that lacks pictures or prices for the product? Would you trust them at their word to get you the product that you want at a fair price, or would you just click away and find another site?

Customers have a right to complain. Why? It's their money. All customers should complain if the quality of either the product or the service is poor. You should complain. We've found most customers are silent complainers. Research shows that only one in 20 customers register their complaints—that's just 4 percent.[1] The other 96 percent take their business elsewhere. Research also shows that complaining customers inform between eight and 10 others about their bad experience. Happy customers tell four or five others, which means that news of a bad experience travels twice as fast. Our research shows that at any given point in time a company has one in four customers with some kind of complaint. It could be a little inconvenience, like when you're in a restaurant and your table isn't prepared with a napkin or a set of silverware. It could be a big problem, like your online product order is now backordered. You won't receive it in time for a birthday gift for a friend, but the company hasn't notified you of the conflict.

Let's tie both of these hypothetical examples together with a real and recent event. Airlines will have weather interference and occasional maintenance delays. These are unavoidable issues, but many other things can compound the problems. For example, one airline announced three plane delays at three adjacent gates almost simultaneously. No explanations had been given except that the planes or crews were late. Their information boards listed the delays before the announcements. Customers were asked to be patient and were told that it would be appreciated. Close to 400 hundred passengers were involved. There weren't enough seats in the concourse for people to sit, so many of them were forced to stand for the entirety of the delay. Each flight had now been delayed for at least an hour. Customers, as you could imagine, were becoming edgy. Many were on the verge of missing connecting flights. The weather outside was sunny, as seen through the windows of the terminal. The agents made an announcement to apologize once more and now added that the delays were due to weather near their flights' destinations. A small serving cart was brought out in an attempt to ease the growing frustration. It looked like it could serve a small party of dinner guests. An agent said on the intercom that guests could help themselves. Soon after, one flight boarded the plane but then unloaded all its passengers a few moments later. The flight had been cancelled. Everyone was instructed to walk to the customer service area on a different concourse to get rebooked. Needless to say, the customer service department was completely overwhelmed with only one agent and a few kiosks with telephones to serve 125 unhappy passengers. Guests were given a $10 voucher for dinner as compensation. This was a nightmare for the customers and an example of disastrous service from the airline.

Why aren't situations like this handled better? Too many companies don't care enough, as evidenced by their procedures and lack of forethought. Too many employees get stuck in the middle of these situations without remedies or assistance. The stress from that kind of pressure can lead many employees to give in to the difficult circumstance and allow their own frustration to influence the already negative situation. That's like adding fuel to a fire.

Employees are part of a company's product. Whether you make the product or you service the customer, how you handle your job significantly affects the customer's experience. It's your job to rise to the occasion when a customer's situation isn't ideal. Will you be able to give aid to someone who may be angry, disappointed, frustrated, annoyed, or even irate? In the airline example, the agents could have done the following to better serve their customers:

▶ Announced the flight delays sooner.

▶ Rephrased how they made their announcements.

▶ Called their supervisor for more assistance.

▶ Provided better compensation.

Superstar customer service is about rising above these kinds of situations and working to make them ideal again for a customer. That's your job. The value of your service will be determined by how well you react to, and ultimately resolve, stressful conflicts. Customers know that some problems can't be avoided. Most customers don't expect perfection. They expect value for their money and a caring approach to solving those problems when they arise.

> *Customers don't expect you to be perfect.*
> *They do expect you to fix things when they*
> *go wrong.*
> —Donald Porter, VP, British Airways

# What Would L.L. Bean Do?

In recent years, Zappos has propelled itself into becoming the largest online shoe retailer in the market. In a recent *Harvard Business Review* blog entry, Bill Taylor detailed Zappos' practice of paying new employees to quit after they've received a week of customer service training if the employee doesn't feel like the company is the right fit for him or her.[1] Zappos wasn't talking small change, either: What initially began with a $100 offer gradually increased to $500, then $1,000. This is a key demonstration on how critical Zappos' employees are to the company's commitment to deliver great service to its customers. It also reveals how transparent Zappos is with its employees. The company readily reveals exactly what it expects out of them, is willing to pay them while it trains them, and then offers everyone $1,000 to leave the job if they don't think they can fully invest themselves in what they are being asked to do. Why does this matter? It shows how far some companies are willing to go to ensure good internal and external customer service, and in doing so achieve enormous success.

An article by Jennifer Ernst Beaudry in *Footwear News* detailed a time when CEO Tony Hsieh was having a vendor meeting when one of his Sketchers reps jokingly suggested that they place a call after hours to Zappos' customer service department and ask for pizza delivery. Hsieh told them to do it. When they called, the customer service representative politely asked the Sketchers rep if he knew he was calling Zappos, the shoe company, and then offered the names of three pizza places that were closest to the caller's location, along with her own personal recommendation.[2]

Zappos isn't the only company that chooses to go above and beyond for its customers. Nordstrom is also famous for its many stories detailing the lengths that it goes to make a customer's experience special. Have you heard of the Nordstrom customer from Portland who wanted an Armani tuxedo for his daughter's wedding? On short notice, the tuxedo was located in New York, shipped to Portland, and altered in time for the important event. Great service, but even more impressive when you learn that Nordstrom doesn't even carry Armani tuxedos. You've undoubtedly heard about the customer who requested a refund for tires that he purchased at a location subsequently purchased by a Nordstrom store. Nordstrom fulfilled his request even though they don't sell tires.

We had a personal experience with a Ritz Carlton in Sydney, Australia, with some misplaced laundry. On an extended business trip, we sent clothing to be laundered through the hotel service. It was not returned at the posted time, and to the dismay of the hotel, they could not locate it. The hotel manager came promptly and apologized profusely. Then he insisted that he be allowed to replace the missing items. He asked how much money would be needed for replacement and offered the cash on the spot. Fortunately, the missing items were located, promptly wrapped, and returned a few hours later. Yet, the hotel refused to accept a refund of the replacement cash.

Fortunately, we could continue to tell you stories of Superstar customer service for many, many pages. And, we would enjoy doing so. There are many wonderful companies, large and small, that pour their heart and soul into countless efforts (some large and some small) to provide magnificent, memorable, heartwarming service for their customers. And, their customers loyally come back time and time again, because they recognize that they will always get what they've paid for and more from these exceptional organizations. Unfortunately, we can also point out many companies that talk the talk, but don't walk the walk. They make promises and go through the motions, and take surveys that suggest they actually care about their customers. But, in the end, it is painfully obvious that their commitment and ability don't really match up. So, what is really required for a company to provide Superstar customer service? Let us give you a snapshot. Note that each element of excellence is described in terms that apply to you, the Superstar customer service representative.

1. **Commit to excellence.** It starts with a commitment to serve the customer. Zappos' Website says, "Powered by Service" right under its logo. Hy-Vee, a powerful employee-owned grocery store in the Midwest, promises "A Helpful Smile in Every Aisle." Bottom line: You need to be bold and declare your stand for excellent service. As a Superstar customer service professional, you bring that promise to life, every day with every customer. You must manage yourself and your commitment first, and then you are in position to positively impact each customer relationship.

2. **Know your business.** Everybody—from the top to the bottom— must know how you fulfill your promise to your customers. The basics, from the quality of the products, to each "customer touch-point" must be understood, practiced, and managed with relentless attention to detail. If you know your business at this level of detail, and can contribute and support each aspect of its continuing pursuit of excellence, you will be recognized as a Superstar.

3. **Make your business systems customer friendly.** If your systems don't help you make your customers happy, they must be fixed or replaced. It's easy to get sucked in to buying or building systems and processes that make our jobs easier. The problem is that the systems and processes often push the customer and their needs aside. Often, senior decision-makers don't see the adverse impacts caused by many business processes. Pay attention to these elements and make them visible in a constructive way to help make them right, and the business will maximize its ability to provide excellence rather than undermine its own efforts.

4. **Hire the right people.** You can't afford anything less than excellent people (from the top to the bottom) who live your commitment to your customers. "Almost" doesn't count. And, "someday" is not soon enough. Zappos' willingness to pay employees who don't "feel it" to leave is a perfect expression of this commitment. If they aren't good enough, pay them to move on so you can find the ones who are. Clearly, this is not the responsibility of the employees on the front lines. You,

however, are positioned to **BE EXCELLENT** on a day-to-day basis, and you're in a position to contribute to a culture of excellence. When each person takes pride in your business and sets a standard that says nothing else is acceptable, the wrong people will stick out like a sore thumb.

5.  **Train everybody.** We have an opportunity to ensure that everyone knows what to do and how to do it. Geoff Colvin, author of *Talent Is Overrated,* says it in many ways. According to Colvin, excellence is a function of time, effort, and focused practice.[3] Training is expensive, but lack of training undermines everything you're trying to accomplish *if* you're really committed to providing excellence. (See number 1.) Each employee need the skills, procedures, and attitudes required for ongoing excellence. Your managers need the skills to lead, coach, redirect, deal with difficult situations, make decisions, and provide support and counsel for long-term service excellence. Often, the best training is provided among peers who are mutually committed to their individual and collective success. Offer to help. Share your knowledge and expertise. Your colleagues will benefit and you will benefit as well.

6.  **Measure everything that matters.** Look for formal and informal indicators that reliably tell you how you're doing and that indicate where you have opportunities to improve. Learn from your supervisors and managers what performance indicators they pay attention to. This helps you to know how to succeed. When you help them achieve the success they're looking for, your success will shine through as well.

7.  **Use your measures to guide you in continuous improvement.** There is always room to improve everything. Enough said.

8.  **Empower your employees**. After your organization has hired the right people, provided the right training, and ensured that each of you is committed and "fits" the culture, you need to act on behalf of the organization's vision of excellence. This means you need information about products and programs, alternatives available to fix customer disappointments, and resources to apologize and compensate for the inevitable screw-ups that companies commit. Learn how problems get solved and you

are positioned to solve them yourself. If you're not sure, check with a manager, but remember that they (managers) prefer it if you will make the right decisions and take care of customers on your own.

9. **Think.** You'll do much better if you build an environment and demonstrate that you care about your customers and employees and that you always want to do better. It's easy to let yourself become cynical and talk trash about employees when they're not within hearing range. This type of thinking becomes toxic, and undermines your willingness to do and be your best. Furthermore, each time another person shares in that conversation with you, it becomes more and more likely that someone who can influence your career will hear and know of your shaky customer commitment. Manage yourself. Think and construct your role as a Superstar, customer by customer, day by day over the long haul. You'll be amazed at where it can take you.

You are capable of providing the exceptional service that the companies we have highlighted provide. With the proper training, engagement, and dedication for performance improvement it is possible to bring your customer service to the next level.

> *Know what your customers want most and*
> *what your company does best. Focus on*
> *where those two meet.*
>
> —Kevin Stirtz

## You Can't Treat Me Like That!

### The Lack of Courtesy, Civility, Manners, and Friendliness

To start, check out these examples. Can you relate to any of them?

**Grocery store:** The checkout clerk scans your order, doesn't acknowledge you, and then turns and talks to a friend about lunch.

**Department store:** You are shopping for clothes and can't find anyone to help. You go and check out at the "customer service" counter, and the clerk is annoyed that you have some questions. You notice she rolls her eyes and sighs.

**Specialty retail:** You buy a sweater online, and it doesn't show up when they said it would. You go to the website and have a hard time finding a number to call. You finally find the number on a distant page, and when you call, you are put on hold for five minutes. You didn't want to send an online message because you have tried that before and never received an answer.

**Fast food restaurant:** You pick up a sandwich and are in line to pay for it. The person in front of you pays. You step up to the counter and the clerk stares at you without saying anything. You say, "This is where you say, 'Can I help you?'" The clerk says, "Oh yeah, can I help?"

**Bank:** You wait in line an intolerably long time and the bank clerk says, "Next. Account number?" without even a "Good morning!" or "How may I help you today?"

**Restaurant:** You are out to dinner with your family. The hostess is friendly but the waitress shows up only after you ask another waitress for help. She curtly asks what you want to order. The service goes downhill from there. She didn't check on you, refill water, ask if you want dessert, or even thank you.

**Computer company:** You have a new personal tablet that freezes frequently. You go online to troubleshoot the problem, but none of the recommendations worked. You call tech support and are put on hold for 20 minutes. Then, the tech person doesn't speak your language well, and you have a hard time understanding his or her instructions. You give up and decide to stop in to the store where you bought it and look for help where you are met with a long line and a wait.

**Government:** You need to renew your license so you stop at a DMV nearby. You wait in line for what seems like forever. When it's finally your turn, the clerk tells you, "You need to fill out the form. Go over there. Next." You get in line again. The clerk takes your form and says abruptly, "Now go in that line over there." The whole experience takes an hour and a half.

**Office supply store:** You need to buy a few supplies including a new printer for your home office. You just finished picking up a few groceries when you run into the office supply store nearby. Someone approaches you immediately and asks if you are in the market for a new laptop, saying he can get you a great deal. You say no, but you need some other supplies including copy paper and ink. He responds, "It is over there." After you find what you are looking for, the clerk at the checkout reminds you about the sale on laptops. You say, "No thank you," and leave with only a few of the items you wanted, not even bothering to look at printers.

**Home improvement store:** You need to buy a new grill for summer cookouts. You like charcoal grills but are considering a more expensive gas grill. You go to the store and head to the outdoor department. No one is around. You starting checking out the small selection of inexpensive charcoal grills, then move on to the more expensive gas grills. After eyeing one of the many gas grills, you see a few employees around, but they don't ask if you need help. You finally flag one over and ask a few questions, only to be met with a smiling, glassy-eyed look. Clearly they know nothing about gas grills. You hurriedly buy the cheaper charcoal grill and get out of there.

## Why? Why? Why?

People today are less civil and kind. Why? Research shows the following reasons:

1.  **Lack of family values and manners.** Teaching children family values and manners isn't being made a priority. Ask any elementary or junior high teacher who has had to deal with an increasing number of impolite students.

2.  **Lack of customer service etiquette.** Businesses don't train their employees in customer service etiquette enough. For proof, go online to Yelp or Angie's List to hear what customers have to say about their service experiences. Or read through one of the many reports put forth by the American Customer Satisfaction Index, which rates businesses on the basis of customer satisfaction.

3.  **Technology.** Businesses focus on technology to serve customers. More and more companies want to drive customers to their Website for purchases or use their automated phone system for customer service, rather than deal with the customer live.

4.  **Entitlement mentality.** We have noticed many articles and books describe a degree of complacency in business today in many aspects of running a company. Worldwide we have lost our competitive describes marked complacency in business today in many aspects of running companies. For example, the United States has lost its competitive edge globally because of a lack of continuous improvement approaches in many areas in business, education, and government.

5.  **Personal responsibility.** In his book *Megatrends,* John Naisbitt projected the future will bring high tech, high touch.[1] Today,

high tech is expanding at a geometric rate. However, we are losing high touch. People skills, civility, friendliness, courtesy, and manners aren't valued as they once were in companies, in families, or by individuals. Moreover, people don't take the personal responsibility for engaging others appropriately. Look at the interactions everywhere from reality television to the political arena. You see more self-centered, backstabbing, and blatant rudeness than ever before. This kind of behavior doesn't win friends or influence people, and it certainly doesn't win customers and keep them for life.

6.  **Rude behavior.** Have you experienced or noticed any of the following?

    ☑ People butting in line.

    ☑ A poor or lack of a greeting.

    ☑ Lack of listening skills.

    ☑ A person who starts talking to someone else when listening to you.

    ☑ People walking in front of you and not saying, "Excuse me."

    ☑ People interrupting your conversation to say what's on their mind.

    ☑ Not offering an elder a seat on the subway.

    ☑ Not offering to let an elder go first in line.

    ☑ Abruptly putting you on hold on the phone.

    ☑ Sarcasm.

    ☑ Dirty jokes.

    ☑ Swearing or other inappropriate language.

    ☑ Treating people differently based on their looks or ethnicity.

    ☑ Expressing biases and prejudices.

    ☑ Criticizing others or the competition.

    ☑ Complaining about their company.

    ☑ People yelling at one another.

    ☑ Not saying please or thank you.

☑ Lack of eye contact.

☑ Ignoring you while you are waiting.

☑ Not apologizing for mistakes.

☑ Fake friendliness in a condescending manner.

☑ Robotic help with a complete lack of sincerity.

If these actions are the norm at an organization and they want to go high tech to take care of their customers, their customer service will always be lackluster. To be a leader as a company, and a Superstar as an individual, you must give the personal care and friendly service.

## You Can't Treat Me Like That!

After reading the examples we started this chapter with, could you add your own examples of poor customer service? Did you find any commonalities from one situation to the next? Oftentimes you'll find that you are generally treated with a lack of courtesy, civility, manners, and friendliness. Customers face it frequently. Following you will find "Moments of Truth" ideas for you use if you are experiencing exceptionally poor, or exceptionally excellent customer service.

**Moment of Truth: Poor Service**—Without being malicious, explain the problems and poor service. Be specific without being cruel or judgmental. The idea lists a link the person or company can go to for a free download on how to provide Superstar customer service as well as a link to our publisher, where they can buy this book.

**Moment of Truth: Superstar Service**—Research says 91 percent of employees like and want more recognition and 50 percent say they never get any at all.[2] We believe in consistent, positive praise and coach all managers in doing so sincerely and regularly. Your next tool is a recognition card. It gives you a place to identify specific actions that you experienced that made them a Superstar! The same links are listed to encourage the individual receiving the card to keep learning and improving on their skills.

With more positive or negative feedback, companies and individuals will get the information they need to improve.

> *People expect good service but few are willing to give it.*
>
> —Robert Gateley

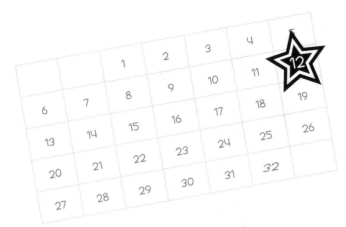

# What You Should Expect From Your Boss, and What to Do When Your Boss Doesn't Do What You Expect

According to research documented in our book *Superstar Leadership: A 31-Day Plan to Motivate People, Communicate Positively, and Get Everyone on Your Side*, 50 percent of managers fail at their jobs. As we mentioned previously, the American Customer Satisfaction Index stated that the average CSI in the US is 76.3—a C, at best, on a test. Unfortunately, most managers, unless they are in customer service or sales, don't pay much attention to customer surveys and feedback. Hopefully, your manager believes in and acts on continuous improvement in customer service for internal and external customers, regardless of your position. What should you expect from your boss? We speak from experience when we share this with you, having helped companies improve their customer experience scores 15 points, reduce complaints more than 60 percent, adding to sales growth improvement by 8 percent, and win 34 quality service awards. We work through managers, giving them a customer experience leadership road map to follow. This road map will take you step-by-step through Plan, Train, Coach, and Renew, all leading to leadership excellence. Your manager needs to be applying these concepts to help you win at customer service.

*Figure 12-1*

## Plan

Your manager needs to give you a plan with clear expectations and goals of the company's customer experience expectations. You need to know your:

▶ CRM (Customer Relationship Management) system.

▶ Key customer profiles.

▶ Customer survey process and data.

▶ Customer service policies (no matter what department you are in).

▶ Customer satisfaction/loyalty goals and plans.

▶ Customer complaint process.

▶ Product knowledge.

▶ Expectations/goals for your role and job.

## Train

To be most effective in your job, you need ongoing training. Companies and managers that provide consistent training for employees outperform the rest. Here are some areas you will want help in:

▶ Job-specific training.

▶ Technical training for your CRM, system software, and your company intranet resources or portals.

▶ Customer service training.

▶ Product knowledge training.

## Coach

We know from experience that the best managers have the best people. Why? They hire smarter, and provide consistent training and coaching. We coach managers to provide weekly to monthly one-on-one coaching sessions with each employee. Why? This process improves communication, reduces problems, increases innovation, and adds to productivity. A one-on-one coaching session usually lasts 30–60 minutes, first asking for your input on strengths, areas for improvement, and ideas, and second, giving feedback and guidance while improving on or building a plan for success. Finally, a coaching session will engage you in a dialogue through this process, and provide ample recognition or praise for work progress and achievement.

## Renew

This is the X factor. A good coach and a Superstar leader guides with integrity and caring, creating a positive and upbeat working atmosphere, holding regular department meetings, and including the team in planning and improvement processes. A good coach will set high standards and do everything he or she can to give the team the tools, support, encouragement, and resources to excel. If you have a good boss, chances are he or she is implementing strategies that include planning, training, coaching, and renewing his or her team of employees. The boss may not be perfect, but is helpful. Revel in this and that person.

## What if Your Manager Doesn't Do This?

As we stated earlier, many times managers won't give you exactly what you need to succeed. That's life. Some say the best leaders have a bit of crazy in them. Nassir Ghaemi, MD, and professor of psychiatry and director of mood disorders at Tuft Medical Center, wrote a book about this called *First Rate Madness.* He cites that leaders in crisis often exhibit mental illnesses.[1] For example, Lincoln, Churchill, King, and Gandhi all had a level of depression. Many so-called "normal" managers are just poor leaders.

Regardless of your boss's erratic behavior, it's not an excuse to do a poor job with customers. Serving the customer with distinction is your job. You can do it well with or without a manager's engagement. It may be a bit more challenging with a bad boss, but Superstars break through those challenges. Superstars and budding Superstars have the conviction to perform extraordinarily well when things are difficult or not. Here are some tips to help you.

## How to Communicate With Your Boss

We have learned in our employee surveys that the number-one characteristic employees hate about their bosses is lack of communication. Make a covenant with yourself to be a model employee. Step one is to learn your job well. Keep learning. Go the extra mile with your customers. Most poor or inept bosses will leave you alone because you are getting the job done. More importantly, this will bolster your pride and self-esteem. A friend had a tree that was burned in a grass fire by his home. He considered chopping it down but instead decided to fertilize it and let it grow. Through time it grew into a tall, beautiful tree that gave his house some awesome shade. Other trees that weren't in the fire didn't grow to the same heights or charm. Sometimes obstacles like having a difficult boss can be good for us.

Step two is to communicate upward about your job and interaction with customers. Bad bosses hate surprises. This starts by making sure you meet with your boss regularly (monthly to quarterly) to review your goals, expectations, and actions steps. We introduced this in Day 2. By making this a regular habit, you are showing initiative, and minimizing misunderstandings about what you are accountable and responsible for in your job. If you wait for your boss to come to you, it's too late. Also, keep your manager updated on important issues and problems with customers so there are no surprises.

Finally, consult others on how they deal with your boss. Your coworkers may have learned some strategies that will help you. Do this discreetly. Don't ask someone, "Hey, Joe is a jerk as a manager. How do you handle him?" Quietly ask others for advice in working with managers, or if a certain scenario ever happened to them and how did they deal with it.

## Manage Your Emotions

Nobody is perfect or immune to the stress of the job, so take care of yourself. Here are a few dos and don'ts.

**Do:**

▶ Manage your own performance so you excel. It tends to take the pressure off.

▶ Take responsibility and accountability for your own success. It's been said, "If it is to be, it's up to me."

▶ Work on your own communication skills so you can relate to people more effectively.

▶ Build your network inside and outside of your company. Go to conferences, chamber meetings, and outside training sessions if you can. It will add to your experience and perspective.

▶ Follow through on personal care activities (diet, exercise, relaxation, vacations, timeouts, etc.) to relieve stress.

**Don't:**

▶ Take a bad boss's behavior personally. It's about him or her. You can't change your boss; you can only change yourself.

▶ Give what you get from your boss. You shoot yourself in the foot and put yourself in his or her category.

▶ Criticize or malign your boss in front of others. It will come back to haunt you at some point.

▶ Give in. You may be forced to confront a bad boss sometime. Do it constructively.

▶ Burn bridges. Keep serving your customer with excellence. Find another job opportunity if you have to, but leave in style.

In summary, you owe it to your customers to do the best job you can regardless of the working environment. If you were your customer what would you want from you? All companies have thousands of moments of truth with customers every day. A moment of truth is anything that companies or employees do that affects the customer perception of the product, service, or employee. Your company's managers put conditions on the type of service they are willing to give based on how they operate the business. Sometimes the conditions are great and other times they aren't because of management decisions. Your job is to provide Superstar customer service by positively managing your moments of truth one customer at a time. You can't handle every customer your company serves, but you can serve the one customer in front of you with care, concern, and commitment.

| Superstar Application |
|---|
| **What does your boss do well?** |
| **What are a few areas you wish your boss could do better?** |
| **What irritates you about your boss?** |
| **What are you doing that may contribute to your boss's challenges?** |
| **What are you willing to change to be a more effective employee and team player?** |

*There is only one boss. The customer. And he can fire everybody in the company from the chairman on down, simply by spending his money somewhere else.*

—Sam Walton, founder, Walmart

## Begin With the Highest Form of Courtesy
### *Are You Listening?*

Superstars are courteous, friendly, and helpful. Are you listening? Listening is the highest form of courtesy, and the baseline for exemplary service is human interaction, treating others with respect, dignity, and care. We mentioned already that poor employee attitudes and a lack of courtesy drive customers away. So ask yourself: Is that something I want for my company?

There are two general approaches when dealing with people and customers. The first is a self-centered approach when relating to people. Your focus is on you, not others. In a self-centered approach, what's most important is what's happening to you and how it affects you. If something doesn't go your way, you get irritated, frustrated, and angry, and let people know. This is the wrong approach for customer service, coming from a lack of maturity or an uncaring attitude. Not caring is a disease that has to be cured.

The second approach is other-centered. Your goal here is to help other people, your customers, or your coworkers. Highly successful and respected businessman Bob Conklin always said, "Help other people get what they want, and you will get what you want." Notice how he said this. First you help, then you get. It is a caring approach when done genuinely and with integrity. In other words, you care how others are affected by your actions, and you wish them well and try to do the right thing for them. This is a prerequisite for Superstar customer service.

To determine whether your approach is self-centered or other-centered, organize your interactions into moments of truth according to the following definitions.

**Moment of Truth:** Anything you do that directly affects customers' perception of *you* (remember: you are the company you work for) or your organization.

**Moment of Misery:** When you do less than the customer expects.

**Moment of Mediocrity:** When you only meet a customer's expectation.

**Moment of Magic** (a term registered by our friend Shep Hepken): When you exceed the customer's expectation.

The goal is to treat customers much better than they expect by self-managing these four moments of truth that help you deliver Superstar customer service. There are five key skills to help you realize these moments of truth.

## 5 Skills to Achieve the Highest Levels of Courtesy and Service

### 1. Mental Psyche: A Positive Way to Stay Positive!

Without a doubt it can be tough to stay positive and deliver the best service. That's why, as customers, we all experience moments of misery or mediocrity nearly every day. Too many service providers succumb to the doldrums of work and provide poor to average service at best. The bad news is it won't necessarily get any better. The good news is that with the right actions, you can make a positive difference with the customers you help. How do you deliver courtesy every day? Just do it, as Nike would say! Mental Psyche is the key! There are three steps:

1. Visualize: See it!

2. Verbalize: Say it!

3. Vitalize: Do it!

The first step to courtesy and great service has nothing to do with the customer. It has everything to do with your attitude and approach. These three steps are essentially what superstar athletes do to become peak performers.

Regardless if things are going well or not, to stay positive you have to work at it. Learn to do these three steps in your mind and you'll become a peak performer. In other words, when an internal or external customer has a request or concern, your goal is to picture success, believe it is important to do, tell the customer that fact, and then take action to get it done. Don't be like so many people who hide behind daily frustrations, policies, procedures, job descriptions, or the like. Great service providers have a motto: Do it now! Anything less is unacceptable.

## 2. The Greeting: Courtesy Is Applied!

Engage all customers respectfully!

▶ Smile and make eye contact.

▶ Be polite.

▶ Be upbeat and positive.

These are keys, aren't they? It's hard to work with a crabby person. In fact, it's irritating. Be the kind of person who plans to make it a better day for every individual you talk to. It's been said that when you help others, you help yourself, so be polite and friendly. After all, isn't that what you want as a customer? It's all about being friendly by proactively helping customers and doing it with a sincere genuine interest to be helpful.

## 3. Meet the Need With Care

Help the customer get what he or she wants, even if he or she is complaining or rude. Not all customers are friendly. Oops! Blasphemy! Did we say that? It's true though, isn't it? Take these actions:

▶ Listen.

▶ Ask questions.

▶ Devise a plan.

▶ Act on it!

After all, why do you have a job? Aside from making money, it is usually to help someone. Get an answer for the customer. If you don't have the answer, find someone who does. For your internal customer, including sales and operations, be a team player for the good of the company and your external customer. Otherwise, you'll lose customers because of petty disagreements, such as who does what. The bottom line is to do something to help and do it today.

### 4. Follow Through Brilliantly

One critical success factor for Superstars is follow-through. This is about taking steps to go the extra mile, such as:

▶ Call back.

▶ Send an e-mail for review.

▶ Do something that was not requested.

▶ Call proactively to check on progress.

▶ Give the customer an update.

▶ Provide an added service or idea.

These types of actions separate the winners from the losers in business every day. Delivering moments of magic for your coworkers and customers alike by doing these things is like adding an exclamation point to the service you give them.

### 5. Handle Problems Positively!

All service and quality breaks down to some degree, and customers will complain about it. Customer complaints don't always have to be viewed as negative; rather they are moments that provide key opportunities to help and change their experience. We talked about handling complaints in Day 9 and will discuss them further in Day 19 and Day 20. Until then, consider these points:

▶ **Deal with the person:** Listen, empathize, and apologize.

▶ **Deal with the problem:** Create a plan, explain it, and do it.

Service organizations will have problems. You can't wish them away. Embrace them and become a solution-finder, not a problem-creator. Remember that delivering moments of magic is a state of being. It's what you do, and it is also who you are. Your goal has to be 100-percent customer loyalty. How are you achieving that today?

A motivational speaker once challenged his audience: "Is there anyone out there that can't get along with others? Please stand up." No one stood. The speaker issued the challenge again, and finally one man stood up in the back. The speaker moved forward on the stage and asked, "Sir, you mean to tell me you can't get along with others?" The man replied, "Sure I can, but I felt sorry for you standing up there alone!"

Everyone feels they get along with others. Unfortunately, the world begs to differ. The world stage shows constant struggles and distant wars between and within nations. Additionally, local news media too often are the spotlight for highlighting crime, family turmoil, gang battlegrounds, school violence, and political bickering. Are people really getting along?

In his books on emotional intelligence, Daniel Goleman identifies the importance of social competence or people skills in career success. He defines empathy as the awareness of others' feelings, needs, and concerns, as well as social skills and adeptness at inducing desirable responses in others. Similar words could be used to describe a Superstar. Check out the brief assessment that follows to gauge your courtesy effectiveness. No matter the results, keep on learning and striving to get better.

---

### Superstar Application: The Superstar Courtesy Check

**Directions:** Rate yourself on your customer-service "people skills" to the degree you engage in the following behaviors. These can apply to internal and external customers. Rate yourself as you think others would.

| 1 = very infrequently | 3 = neutral |
| 2 = infrequently | 4 = frequently |
| 5 = very frequently. | |

Put your rating in the space to the right of each item.

| | |
|---|---|
| 1. Smiling while you work | |
| 2. Making eye contact in conversations | |
| 3. Expressing a positive welcome to customers on the phone or in person | |
| 4. Listening effectively | |
| 5. Summarizing your understanding of a customer's need | |
| 6. Understanding others' needs before sharing your ideas | |
| 7. Demonstrating manners by saying please, thank you, excuse me, etc. | |
| 8. Helping others based on their needs | |

| Superstar Application: The Superstar Courtesy Check | |
| --- | --- |
| 9. Recognizing the positive input of others | |
| 10. Offering added service or help | |
| 11. Using verbal or non-verbal cues in communication | |
| 12. Remembering to say thank you | |
| 13. Treating all people with respect, courtesy, and dignity | |
| 14. Valuing diversity in people | |
| 15. Communicating without biases and prejudices | |
| 16. Creating teamwork with others | |
| What are 2–3 strengths? | |
| What are 1–2 areas to improve? | |

*Revolve your world around the customer and more customers will revolve around you.*

—Heather Williams

## You Are Going to Have to "Gotta Wanna" Lead Yourself to Success

Robots have become the wave of the future—mechanical or virtual agents devoid of feeling and emotion, programmed to do repetitive tasks. Have you ever encountered someone who gave you robotic customer service? What did you think about the quality of their service? Did you want to rush out and get back to that store or restaurant? Robotic service can arise in any workplace. The most overridingly common characteristic is doing just enough to get the job done and no more. A poster we came across summarizes this perfectly. The photo showed a serene forest. Written directly below it was the word *Motivation*. The caption read, "If a motivational poster is all it takes to fire you up, you probably have an easy job, the kind robots will be doing soon." Success is really a do-it-yourself project, and it takes more effort than "just enough" to be great. You have to "gotta wanna" be a Superstar.

Have you ever felt like you weren't making any progress in your job? Have you felt like you go three steps forward but take two steps back? Let's face it: Customers complain, technology breaks down, managers get upset or let you down, your friends don't support you, products have quality problems, and your company changes. You can choose to become frustrated, confused, and tired. Or, you can choose to achieve more career advancement, recognition for a job well done, and job satisfaction. How do you break through to achieve all of this?

## Understanding a Breakthrough: A Struggle That Never Ends

In every person, there's a combination of right and wrong thinking. For the purposes of this chapter, right thinking means what works and wrong thinking refers to what doesn't. For every dream, there's darkness; for any ounce of confidence, there's an equal amount of doubt; for every mountain of hope, there's a valley of despair. Similarly, for every good thing that happens at work, there seems to be an equal amount of potential bad. Too often, people let the wrong thoughts dominate their thinking, or they let the right thoughts pass by unnoticed. Which pattern will control one's life? Which will prevail? Right thinking, and therefore right living, is like golf: Hit a few good shots, and you feel great, but once you flub a few, your concentration and confidence slip. In the world of customer service, these forces are always present, and how you handle them determines how good you will be.

Right thinking and acting are crucial to customer service. They have to be worked at again and again. In the world of customer service, there's unlimited opportunity to do well. Yet, many well-intentioned people fall short of their potential. To some people, the idea of doing their jobs with care and providing customer service or sales can seem foreign, particularly when it comes to applying these principles daily. It is one thing to talk it, and it's another thing to walk it every day. Their negative habits and bad memories from the past stop them in their tracks. However, there are a few enlightened people who learn a better way and are propelled toward success. In spite of obstacles, their vision of professional customer service is brilliantly executed, which attracts customers and attention from all angles. Think of the salmon that swims upstream every year to spawning waters. The trip is difficult and often fatal, but an inner belief drives them forward to their goal. Isn't every experience in life a possible victory or failure? As Shakespeare said, it's your choice: "Nothing is good or bad, except thinking makes it so."

## How to Break Through

Think of a time in your life when you did your best work. You handled that key account with care, helped a friend in need, or romanced your spouse or significant other. How did you feel? How did time pass? You might have been elated, satisfied, happy, and energized. Time most likely passed without notice. Now, think of a time in your life when you did poor work, neglected your friends, or argued with someone. How did you feel? How did time pass? You might have felt rejected, disgusted, sad, or exhausted. Time most likely moved at a snail's pace. Any of the situations recalled have a number of common characteristics. First, your mind was filled with thoughts about each experience. Second, you experienced feelings—good, bad, or indifferent. Third, the passing of time was as constant as the heavens, although you may not have experienced it that way. And fourth, you responded in each experience. What did you do during and after each experience? That is the key to Superstar customer service and the golden ticket to leading yourself to success and excellence. Did you reach up and pull down the best there is to offer, or did you curl up in a ball and let the world push you along? When things didn't work out, you may have focused on the problem and took minor action, if any. But, when things triumphed, you probably envisioned all of the possibilities and let the creativity flow. You had right thoughts about the experience, and then you took action to make positive things happen, rather than lashing out in fear, frustration, or disgust. What you think, you become! It's always pure choice.

Professionally and personally, your greatest gift is your ability to choose your thoughts and actions. We must do this in good times and bad to be true champions in life. How? Take a break, and think, review your goals, remind yourself of your purpose in difficult situations, and remember to focus on the customer's point of view and needs. Think about what the right thing to do is. By learning to think right, you'll do what's right more often. Once you do, you possess the ability to break through what holds you back from achieving Superstar status in your work.

## Superstars: Thinking Right and Acting Right

A prophet was on a hill one day. He told his followers, "I quit." They were aghast and cried out that they needed him and they would do anything for him; they would die for him. The prophet smiled and requested, "Live joyously." But the followers put their heads down and walked away slowly. That was too hard to do. All they wanted was to talk and dream about it. If you're not willing to take action, you're no better than the man who starved in a kitchen full of food because he didn't have the sense to cook it.

Customers will define what's right for them. By listening and paying careful attention to them, you'll know the right actions to take. That's the only way to overcome objections, rejections, complaints, and dissatisfaction. Do your work with a smile. Be polite and say thank you. Think innovatively about how you can help customers and add value as you work with them. Solve problems, quickly and kindly. Work cooperatively. Ultimately, give customers the value they deserve.

A frog once let a scorpion hitch a ride on his back to get across the stream. Somewhere along the way, the scorpion stung the frog. The frog cried, "Why did you do that? Now we'll both drown." The scorpion replied, "I don't know. I guess it's just in my nature." What's your nature? Is it to be positive or negative in your efforts to do your job? Or, are you just in it for a paycheck? You will generate premier results by choosing the right thoughts and actions. You will make a difference!

Successful people do the right things and it pays off in income, success, and happiness. Can *you* think right to do right, like other successful people? Would you agree that it's right to help people rather than hinder them? Or care for your loved ones rather than neglect them? To take action, rather than worry all the time? Give rather than steal? Praise rather than criticize? Be positive rather than negative? Or love rather than hate? The answer is yes to all of these questions, isn't it? In customer service, what we're talking about are actions like listening, helping, cooperating, being positive, and caring. But in order to take action, you must first think. Thought always precedes action. William James said, "The greatest discovery of our generation is that we can alter the outer aspects of our lives by changing the inner attitudes of our mind."

By "thinking right," you can live right by taking right actions. Ultimately, it's not about right or wrong; it's about a mindset that works to lead you to success.

> *The more you engage with customers the*
> *clearer things become and the easier it is to*
> *determine what you should be doing.*
>
> —John Russell, president,
> Harley Davidson

## Problem-Solving Your Way Through the Forest

Without problems, customer service would be obsolete. As the late Dr. Norman Vincent Peale once declared, "The more problems you have, the more alive you are. The only people without problems are six feet under." To a certain extent, you want problems so you have customers to serve. Though the logic may sound counterintuitive, problems generate excellent customer service opportunities that not only help the customer that day, but also can reinforce their loyalty in your company long-term.

To better understand customers' problems and problem-solving techniques, and to help better engage and serve your customer, it is first important to look at the fundamental reason that problems exist.

### Why Do Customers Have Problems?

Customers have problems for a variety of reasons. On any given day, you may have a customer who simply is having a bad day and is in a bad mood, or you may meet a customer with a company-based issue. No matter where it began, typically complaints fall into one of the following categories:

1. Product didn't work properly.

2. Product was different than what was represented.

3. Service was poor quality.

4. Service was not as promised.

5. Employees not helpful or knowledgeable.

6. Employees were rude or discourteous.

Not every customer expresses a concern or complaint every time. Why? They don't want take the time or don't care that much about a perceived issue. Look at your own past behavior; do you complain every time when you have an issue? Our research with customer surveys with clients and potential has shown that at any given point in time, 25 percent of customers have some kind of complaint, big or small, with every company.

Customers have different standards and expectations that influence their decision to express a problem. Many times, a customer is irrational and unpredictable. Problem "A" today may not be an issue tomorrow. The difference between pleased and displeased could simply be the customer's mood or life circumstances at the time. No matter the circumstance, if customers feel there is a problem they have a right to communicate it. You and your company have the obligation to try to help them.

Differentiating between problems and complaints is key in helping get them resolved. A mechanical engineer is solving problems when designing new parts with a customer. The engineer is listening to a complaint when a customer gives an impassioned speech about the lack of courtesy shown to him or her by the salesperson. An architect designs a building for a customer to solve a problem or meet a need. He or she addresses a complaint when the customer talks about feeling constantly ignored and left out of the design process. Many times, complaints are rooted in emotion and perception, whereas problems aren't as fluid and have a more solid basis. Resolving both problems and complaints is important in maintaining a good relationship with your customer.

The top performers in the customer service industry use a system or process to guide their problem-solving skills. When confronted with problems, consider the problem-solving process as described here.

## The Problem-Solving Process

▶ **Identify the facts.** Determine the specifics of the situation. Hard Data: numbers, dates, stats, or time frames. Soft Data: feelings, opinions, personalities, or behaviors.

▶ **Problem statement.** Clearly and specifically identify the problem.

I► **Possible solutions.** Identify three alternative solutions and the possible outcomes.

I► **Recommended solution.** Decide on a course of action. You may need to use or try the other solutions later.

I► **Action steps.** Specifically create a plan and a timeline to implement the solution.

For example, consider this scenario:

*A company hastily began to sell a much-needed new product. After a couple of months of sales, results were poor. Many felt that not enough time was given for the product to catch on and that more promotion would do the trick and increase sales.*

*The customer relationship manager at the organization used the problem-solving process to deal with the issue and craft a solution. She began gathering facts by listening to customer complaints, visiting with the business partners in the field, and talking to her customer service reps. She learned that by quickly rolling out the product, customer service reps and business partners lacked knowledge to adequately demonstrate the product and to answer customer questions. The problem was the lack of product knowledge at the sales rep and field level not a marketing or advertising issue. She presented her findings to the vice president of sales and marketing using the format outlined here. Reps were divided into three groups to receive three training sessions over the next month. The training focused on product knowledge and handling objections. The business partners provided Webinars to learn the features and benefits of the product, too. Field reps then made on-site visits to further answer questions and to help with demos. Results improved dramatically.*

When dealing with customers, this problem-solving process can be done in an involved basis, like the one just demonstrated. Or it may be done in a few minutes on the phone or in person. One client we work with has a service center devoted to these brief problem-solving sessions. Guests or hotel staff call the service center team with questions or problems related to the guests' accommodations and their hotel experience. Calls usually last from a few minutes to an hour, depending on the issue.

Another client that services thousands of businesses in the United States and Canada sends customer service reps (CSRs) to deliver products on a weekly basis, offer other products, and deal with any issues or problems. The CSRs are empowered to serve the customer and problem-solve how to help them on the spot on a daily basis. If they can't solve the problem, it moves up to the manager.

An effective problem-solving process and the skills to support it are crucial in either case. To help you collaborate with customers or co-workers to solve any issue, use some of these Superstar communication techniques.

## Communication Techniques

**Open-ended questions:** Including what, where, when, why, and how. The purpose is to engage the customer in a dialogue so they describe their need, issue, or complaint. Ask:

» What symptoms you are experiencing?

» Where did this take place?

» When does this occur?

» Why do you think there is an error?

» How did you try to fix it?

**Closed-ended questions:** Used to identify specifics, gain agreement, and focus on a solution by limiting options. They are usually answered with yes or no, or facts or figures. Ask things like:

» Is it making a noise?

» Did you follow steps 1–5?

» Have you rebooted it yet?

» Would you like me to review the warranty?

» Are you gaining any power now?

**Directives:** To get your customer to discuss things further, say things like:

» Tell me more about that.

» Can you give me an example?

» Describe what happens.

**Paraphrase:** To make sure you know what the customer is asking, say things like:

» What I hear you saying is...

» I understand you to say....

» To summarize, what's happening is....

**Verbal Cues:** Verbal cues are important to bring into the conversation to help keep discussion going. Add things like:

⏩ I see.

⏩ Okay.

⏩ What else?

**Non-Verbal Cues:** Non-verbal cues help the customer know you are attentive and concerned about their issue. They include:

⏩ Eye contact.

⏩ Nodding your head.

⏩ Taking notes.

Problem-solving is an essential part of your job. Sometimes it's a quick process; other times it requires intricate investigation and thought. It can be a proactive process related to a positive outcome the customer is aspiring to reach, or a reactive process regarding a complaint or concern with your company's product or service. No matter the circumstance, you are accountable and responsible to deal with the problem admirably and professionally.

> *Statistics suggest that when customers complain, business owners and managers ought to get excited about it. The complaining customer represents a huge opportunity for more business.*
>
> —Zig Ziglar

## Time Management
### "Who" and "What" Are Both Important Hear (Yes, We Mean H.E.A.R.)

Over nine decades ago, Dr. Evan O'Neill Kane of New York's Kane Summit Hospital felt doctors were losing too many customers in appendectomies, many because of the effects of general anesthesia. He felt that local anesthesia would be better for the customer but, not surprisingly, no volunteers came forward to test his hypothesis. That is until February 15, 1921, when he finally performed an appendectomy with local anesthesia—on himself! In the process, he changed accepted medical practice. To be your best, you often need to change your plan as Dr. O'Niell Kane did; sometimes that change means operating on yourself. Begin analyzing your own situation by simply counting the how many times the letter "f" appears.

FEATURE FILMS ARE THE RESULT

OF YEARS OF SCIENTIFIC STUDY

COMBINED WITH THE

FORMAL EXPERIENCE OF YEARS

How many did you get? 3? 4? 5? 6? There are actually 7! If you missed some, ask yourself why? Why would anyone miss an "f," or two or three, when they are laid out right in front of you? The answer lies in our mental models, the way we perceive things and act on them. Similarly, what you are missing in terms of performance improvement is most likely right in front of you. Sometimes the solutions to your challenges are there, but you just don't see them. Why? Because of entrenched habits, perceptions, and beliefs. When you try to improve, it seems as futile as trying to become 7 feet tall when you are fully grown at 6 feet. Your mental models mostly work to keep you in your comfort zone unless you change your thinking through new learning or experiences. Let's try it again. Read the following phrases out loud that are written in the triangles. Read them fast. Ready, go!

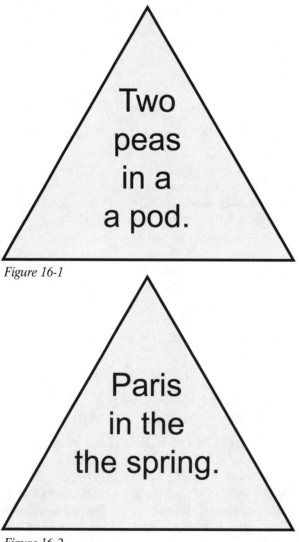

*Figure 16-1*

*Figure 16-2*

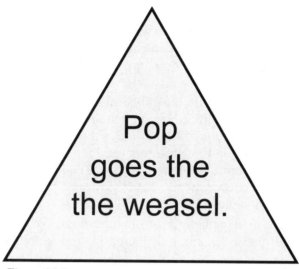

*Figure 16-3*

Notice each has an extra word—a, the, the. Did you catch on to what was happening? Most people don't see this the first time.

It takes consistent effort to change. Talent, information, and desire are not enough to be successful in time management. Change in self-perception and behavior is required, especially in implementing time-management techniques. Don't let the idea of change intimidate you; big changes aren't usually required. It's the little changes that begin to make a difference.

So, what are you missing that is right in front of you? Sometimes it's solutions to present problems, ideas, and answers to future issues. It can often be attributed to the blinders you put on caused by the beliefs you've learned over the years. Be careful of these self-talk phrases or similar ones:

- *I can't change!*

- *I am what I am!*

- *I'm not that kind of person.*

- *That's me.*

- *I always do it this way; it has worked before.*

Superstar customer service providers have their problems; however, they are more willing to change or try new things if it will get results. If it makes sense, they will shed old habits and beliefs as easily as leaves fall from trees in the autumn.

## Increase Your Productivity

There are 168 hours in any given week. Though you cannot control the number of hours in a week, you can control how you spend those hours. Successful time management requires you to be open to new ways to get more done in less time.

Most people who deal with the public and give customer service spend too much time putting out fires. Not enough time is spent on listening, following up, being of further assistance, and adding value. Your true payoff activities involve these kinds of customer service functions. Be a pro; make the time to get them done. Eliminate the word *can't* and, in the words of Winston Churchill, "never, never, never give up." To begin, remember these important principles:

▶ True time management is self-management. We believe there is no self-improvement, only increasing in the ability to be all that you already are. You can't change others, but you can change yourself.

▶ To take care of customers more effectively you must be willing to change some habits to increase productivity.

▶ A foundation of time management is to respond to all events based on your goals and priorities, rather than reacting to spot urgencies, problems, or needs.

▶ Mind and body are intricately intertwined; to control what you do, better control what you think.

Just like a champion athlete systematically, physically, and mentally prepares to win the gold, customer service Superstars must do the same. Know your product, learn better techniques to be customer centered, and understand how to be ready mentally every day to be your best. HEAR what we are saying about how to be more successful. Consider this acronym to more effectively hear your customers and help them in the time you have to serve them.

**H**armonize

**E**ffectiveness, not efficiency

**A**wareness

**R**esolution

## Harmonize

There is nothing worse than making promises to customers that you don't keep because you forgot to follow through. Blend your energy, ideas, and activities with your coworkers and customers. Be organized so you can implement a coordinated approach to tracking customer interactions as well as managing your time, schedule, and goals. The Franklin Planner is probably the most well-known time-management system. Today, most people use their cell phones or computers for time management. Some companies provide CRM (Customer Relationship Management) software programs to assist you with customer analytics, organization, and tracking. No matter how you choose to keep track of your time, make sure these key elements are included in any system you use consistently for your personal organization:

- ▶ Yearly overview calendar.
- ▶ Monthly overview calendar.
- ▶ Daily calendar (to-do list, calls, and appointments).
- ▶ Telephone log.
- ▶ Customer tracking.
- ▶ Goals and plans.
- ▶ Notes.

Find one approach and use it. Don't use two or three; you'll be ineffective. Also, if it's important, write it down (meeting, ideas, activity, and goal). Initiate this concept in a personal planner, and you'll literally save an hour a day.

## Effectiveness, Not Efficiency

Effectiveness is doing the right things. Efficiency is doing things right. In other words, Superstars focus on assisting customers so they stay loyal customers. This means you invest more time in helping customers and less time in anything else. The goal is how to creatively keep a customer interested, not necessarily to follow procedures to the letter. We have defined the difference between Superstar customer service and simply good service.

Often that difference is the empathy and care you use to do your job. Recently, on a business trip, we saw this amplified in two dinners over two nights. Both places were nice restaurants. The first night the food was good but the waitress really lacked any personal connection with us. She really didn't want to be working and we could tell. The second night the food was good, but the waiter seemed to engage us with a bit of flair and energy. He wanted to be doing his job that night. Guess who received the bigger tip?

## Awareness

Analyze your time effectiveness. What do you do well? How can you improve? Keep learning. If you are a manager, what feedback do you get back from employees that can help you help them serve customers better? If you are in sales, what do your customers tell you—good or bad? If you are in IT, what kind of feedback on your programs or solutions do you get from coworkers or your frontline employees? What feedback do you receive from customer surveys? If your company has various metrics, what can you learn from them? Remember: This is a do-it-yourself project to rise above the crowd. Your goal isn't to be "good enough"; you can be better than that.

## Resolution

The bottom line is all about results and reputation. Do you help the customers with their problems and make them feel better about you and your company so they come back? Do you feel good about it? If you do a great job but hate the work in the long-term you and your customers will suffer. There needs to be a level of integrity present while you are at your job. During a presentation at a company we worked with recently this type of job integrity was demonstrated fully. During a Superstar customer service presentation, we described examples about Superstar performers. We were interrupted by everyone almost unanimously saying, "What about Chris?" We replied, "Who is Chris?" We were informed that Chris was their top customer service manager who had the reputation and results of a Superstar. Chris brought a level of integrity and energy to work every day, and applied it sincerely, and was known for it. After acknowledging Chris we added that, as Sly and the Family Stone said, "Everybody is a star." That's what we believe the potential is for you and others you work with. *You* do have to execute and deliver results for your company products and services while creating a personal reputation that resounds in your industry and workplace. Sum up this day with a review in what we call the Best of the Best Exercise. Write it out or do it mentally. What can you learn to help you become a customer service Superstar?

## Superstar Application: Best of the Best

Think of a time in your career when you did your best work ever. Choose a situation that exemplifies your highest customer service performance. Get a clear mental picture of the event. Replay it in your mind as if it were a movie. Think of the details: people, problems, sounds, feelings, and surroundings. Review in your mind what happened, how you behaved, what you felt and achieved. Capture your thoughts in the space that follows.

Briefly describe the situation.

What was your motivation to succeed or act?

How did you feel?

| Superstar Application: Best of the Best (continued) |
|---|
| What key behaviors or strategies did you use? |
| What lessons can you learn or relearn about your best performance? |

By learning to replicate that experience and improving the result, you will deliver Superstar customer service. To be the best you can be, make a commitment to personal development and excellence. If you want to be exceptional, do exceptional things. The difference between winners and losers is that the winners do what losers won't do at all or won't do enough. Never forget that success is not accidental.

> *Consumers are statistics. Customers are people.*
>
> —Stanley Marcus

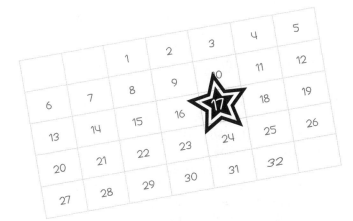

## Etiquette on the Phone, in Electronic Communications, and Face-to-Face

### What Do You Mean, I Get Paid to Be Nice?

Alexander Graham Bell invented the telephone in 1876. Ever since then it has become an indispensable communication tool. With the advent of smartphones, communication has been revolutionized. Superstar customer service means you also have Superstar telephone and e-mail skills.

Let's look at all of the phone mistakes that irritate customers. How often have you come across these scenarios or similar situations?

☐ The person answers the phone after 29 rings and says, "Hello, Jim speaking. Can you hold?" Then puts you on hold immediately.

☐ You call a company's 1-800 number to buy a product and the phone rings and rings. You get an automatic message that puts you on hold and gives you an estimate waiting time of five minutes.

☐ You call a home improvement store and ask if they have a particular product in stock and the person says to wait a minute. You are put on hold forever until he or she returns only to say the store doesn't have it.

☐ You call a credit card company to check on your balance. You have to go through five options or more to get to what you want. Because you have a question, you have to start all over again and wait on hold to talk to a live person.

☐ You call your healthcare provider about payment on a bill. You are transferred three times to get to the finance department. They put you on hold and you get cut off.

☐ You leave a message on voice mail and never hear back from the person you called.

What do you think? How would you react as a customer? Would you like it or complain about it? Would you just ignore it because you have seen it before? In each of these situations the employees are delivering awful service. The companies are in danger of losing customers and adding to a negative word-of-mouth campaign from disgruntled customers. Companies spend millions on advertisements (TV, radio, Internet, newspaper, direct mail) to get customers to buy. But, it only takes one phone call, a few minutes of time at the most, to lose the customer. *You* can change that by handling the phone like a Superstar.

---

### Top 10 Mistakes to Avoid When Handling the Phone

1. Negative, discourteous, rude behavior.

2. Not turning off your phone in a meeting.

3. Answering the phone inappropriately and putting some on hold right away.

4. Talking about business or personal things in the wrong places.

5. Letting the cell phone interrupt other phone or face-to-face conversations.

6. Inappropriate ring tones for a business setting.

7. Criticizing others while on the phone.

8. Unprofessional or outdated voice-mail message.

9. Not following up on your messages in a timely manner.

10. Transferring or putting customers on hold incorrectly and losing the call.

   Bonus: Texting, dialing, or surfing the Net while driving. Please never do this.

## How to Handle the Phone Professionally

It only takes a few moments of truth done positively to make a good impression on the phone. This involves:

1. An initial greeting.

2. Announcing your company.

3. Identifying yourself.

4. Offering to be of service.

It is ideal to answer the phone in three rings or less. Why? Because then your customer doesn't have to wait too long. Waiting time often seems longer on the phone than in person. If you can't do this and you know the customer has had many rings, apologize. Then add, "Good morning!", "Good afternoon!", or "Good evening!"

The next three parts go together. Announce your company or department with a phrase like, "Good afternoon. Superstar Company Name." Then add, "This is Rick. How may I be of service to you?"

So, let's put it all together:

▶ *Good afternoon. Wonderful Company. This is Maria. Where may I direct your call?*

▶ *Good morning. Customer Service. I am Bill. How may I be of service today?* (Or, *How may I help you?*)

## Asking Questions

Part of doing a good job on the phone is asking questions of the customer to understand what they want or need. For example:

You: "Good Evening, Gordon Company, this is Bill. How can I be of service?"

Customer: "I can't seem to figure out how to make this thing operate right."

(You have to ask a few questions because you don't know what he or she is really talking about.)

You: "It sounds like you are a frustrated with a purchase you made recently. I apologize that you are having difficulty. I want to help. In order to help, may I ask you a few questions?"

Open- and closed-ended questions will help decipher exactly what the customer needs.

Use open-ended questions to gather more information. Here are a few examples:

▶ What happened next?

▶ Why do you think that?

▶ How has it responded?

Use closed-ended questions to zero in on facts or gain agreement. Typically they are yes or no questions, such as:

▶ Do you have further concerns?

▶ Can you give me an example?

▶ Has this been helpful?

Good questions get customers to talk openly about their situation. It helps you to build empathy as you listen to them and figure how you can help them.

Let's review some examples.

Let's say the customer wants to check on her order. You ask, "Do you have your order number with you?" The answer will be yes or no. Or, you could ask, "Can you give me your name and account number, and I will check on it for you?" The answer will be yes and the information you asked for. These questions are closed-ended.

In another situation, let's say the customer needs some technical assistance for his smartphone. You may ask, "What you have done so far to try to fix the problem? What happens when you (name of action or activity)?" Notice how in this situation, the customer needs to explain or give more information. These questions are open-ended.

Both of these types of questions can be helpful on the phone or in person. Use open-ended questions at the beginning of the phone conversation to learn more about the problem. Use closed-ended questions to zero in on the specifics related to the problem and to gain agreement with the customer.

## Other Key Phone Skills

Other skills to upgrade to deliver Superstar customer service on the phone include:

▶ Transferring calls.

▶ Taking messages.

▶ Initiating customer calls.

▶ Leaving a message for a customer.

▶ Returning a customer call.

▶ Using e-mail to support your phone contacts.

## Transferring Calls

Learn to transfer calls professionally. Too many customer service people make two big mistakes. They transfer a customer without warning—this is rude—or they don't update the other person that will receive the transferred call about the customer's need. This irritates customers because they have to start all over. Consider these guidelines to do a better job:

▶ Know your system and how to transfer. Most phone systems have unique and different options. So get help, study, and practice how to do it right.

▶ Once you answer a call, if it isn't your job to solve the customer's problem at that point, ask the name of the caller, use it, and ask if he can hold while you transfer him. "Who is calling, please? Mr. Johnson, can you hold while I transfer you?"

▶ Put the person on hold. Connect with the other person and explain what you know. Then connect the call.

▶ Appropriately transfer the call. Many systems allow you to stay on the call for an introduction to the next person.

## Taking Messages

Most calls are transferred into voice-mail today, so you might not need to take many messages. Superstars learn anyway. Your goal is to take an accurate, complete message. Gather the following material:

▶ First and last names of the person.

▶ Company or organization, if appropriate.

▶ Phone number and area code, and extension if it applies.

▶ Brief description of the need.

▶ Date and time of call.

▶ Sense of priority.

▶ Best time to call back, if appropriate.

▶ Signed (by the person taking the message).

Your job may require you to take messages regularly or only on occasion. Regardless, it is important to take accurate and complete information, and to get it to the intended person as immediately as possible.

Did you ever not get a message that you should have? Did you ever receive an incomplete message? How did you feel? We don't want customers to have that experience or feel that way.

## Initiating Customer Calls

In some cases, your job may require you to call the customer first. In other words, you initiate the call. Reasons for these kinds of calls could be to:

▶ Follow up on an order.

▶ Make a sales call.

▶ Do a customer survey.

▶ Schedule an appointment.

▶ Review warranty information.

▶ Collect money.

It all depends on your job.

To make effective customer calls, you have to have good time management. If you handle incoming calls, this is even more important. Incoming calls are reactive. You may know they are coming, but you aren't always sure how many and what they are about.

You need to schedule your outgoing calling time. Why? To achieve priorities, you schedule to get them done. Block the time on your daily schedule that interferes less with your incoming calls and gives you best chance to reach your customers.

Next, be prepared. Organize your notes about your customers on your desktop or laptop. Most companies have a CRM system online to help you. If yours doesn't, use a file folder system. It is equally important to know your product, have all of your literature, rehearse your approach, and keep learning. You will make progress and win more than you lose. That's what Superstars do. If you don't do this, you are taking the mediocre approach.

Make sure you are clear on your goal for your calls. Here is an outline for an effective outgoing call:

▶ Greet the customer, using his or her name.

▶ Identify yourself and your company. Ask if it is a good time to talk. This is called "taking the curse off the call." If it isn't a good time, ask to schedule a better time.

▶ Explain why you are calling.

▶ Help the customer or make your offer.

▶ Summarize all agreements and decisions.

▶ Give the customer your contact information.

▶ Establish a follow-up process and say thank you to the customer.

Here's how you could put it all together:

*Good morning, Mr. Rodriquez. This is Natalie Connor from AZT Stores. How are you today?... Great. Is this a good time to talk?... The reason I am calling is that I wanted to ask you a few questions about your recent visit, which will only take a few minutes. My first question is.... Thank you for taking the time today, and I will pass on your comments about our customer service desk. If you need to reach me for any reason my name again is...and my number is.... Have a nice day.*

## Leaving a Message for a Customer

Very few business calls get through today. Research says only one out of four calls get a live person.[1] Most go to an assistant or to voice-mail. Here are a few suggestions for leaving a message:

▶ Identify yourself and your company.

▶ Speak as normally as possible. Slow down and speak clearly.

▶ Leave your phone number (repeat it slowly) and the best to time to reach you. Then repeat your phone number.

▶ Keep your message brief.

▶ Give your customer one thing you want them to do as a result of the call.

▶ Leave the date and time you called.

▶ Be positive and upbeat, and repeat who you are.

## Returning a Customer Call

Return all customer calls promptly and immediately. One salesperson we knew of at IBM promised to return all calls with four hours. Your promise may need to be even better than that. Superstars find ways to beat the competition.

By the way, keep your voice-mail message up to date. Don't have wrong dates or times on the message; it's unprofessional. Also, as you return calls, delete your messages. Have you ever called someone and a voice-mail prompt said, "This extension is full"? This is unprofessional as well.

Follow similar guidelines to initiating customer calls but add, "I am returning your call," or "I am following up on your message."

## Using E-Mail to Support Your Phone Contacts

Everybody uses e-mail today. Worldwide, more than 2 billion people use e-mail, and the number is growing. More than 300 billion e-mails are sent every day. In 1998 30 percent of people in the US and Canada had email access. Today, more than 80 percent of people have access through desktops, laptops, iPads, or smartphones.[2]

People have access to e-mail nearly everywhere they go: restaurants, coffee shops, airplanes, hotels, businesses, TVs, and in their cars.

Learn to send professional e-mails and use them to add value. Don't become part of the noise and spam. Add value by following up on a customer request, to confirm agreements with customers, when requesting information from customers, when updating customers on your progress, when sending customers valuable information, and to thank customers for business.

Here's how to write a dynamic e-mail that differentiates you professionally and positively:

▶ Define a specific subject (e.g., "Warranty Information on XYZ Television" or "Order Follow-Up for Your Purchase on date/time").

▶ Give a greeting.

▶ Outline what you want or need in the body of the e-mail.

▶ Include bullets on key points.

▶ Close with an appropriate salutation.

▶ Add a P.S. to give value.

▶ Include an appropriate attachment.

Here is an example:

> To: Ljones@nccc.com
>
> From: Bill.Smith@stp.com
>
> Subject: Order Confirmation
>
> Attached: Receipt
>
> Hi Loren,
>
> I hope you are well.
>
> Based on our discussion today at 2:30 p.m., I have taken care of these issues for you:
>
> 1. Current order accuracy.
> 2. Warranty issues.
> 3. Next month's orders.
>
> Attached are the receipts I mentioned. Let me know if you have any questions. Take care.
>
> Sincerely,
>
> Sue
>
> XYZ Company
>
> 223-332-0101
>
> P.S. I look forward to speaking with you and appreciate your patience while I have researched your concerns.

You'll notice this e-mail is longer than most; it is more professional and impressive to customers. Too many e-mails go out that are just a few words, are caustic in tone, lack a subject, and aren't signed.

In summary, these telephone and e-mail skills represent a professional and positive approach. Few people do them all well. Superstars do.

> *Here is a simple but powerful rule: always give people more than what they expect to get.*
>
> —Nelson Boswell

## How to Deal With That *ss***e

Some customers are more difficult than others. When we do customer service training, the three most often asked questions are:

1.  How do you deal with the irate *ss***e or difficult customer?
2.  How do you say no?
3.  How do you handle complaints?

So, we will deal with each of these during the next three days. Let's start with the difficult customer. To begin, we want to establish a new rule for customer service. Many companies have the following "2 Rules of Customer Service" etched in a plaque and on their walls. Many make it the primary tenet of their customer service philosophy. They are:

> **Rule #1:** **The Customer Is Always Right**
> **Rule #2:** **If the Customer Is Wrong, Re-Read Rule #1**

We don't believe in that. Why? Customers are, many times, wrong. Some customers try to cheat you. Others are rude, mean, and irate, and use nasty, colorful words to describe their feelings. Many times these feelings have nothing to do with your service or product, and more to do with their poor behavior and philosophy of life.

Instead, we have developed one edict of customer loyalty. People who receive *customer service* don't necessarily like you or come back. What companies really need is customer loyalty. A loyal customer is one who keeps coming back and becomes an unpaid disciple in spreading the good news about you or your company.

> **Superstar Customer Service Edict:**
> *You Earn Customer Loyalty One Customer at a Time!*

We have already established that the customer is your top priority. In the two previous rules, when the customer is wrong, it implies the employee is also wrong. So an employee has to do the wrong thing to make it right. The customer wins, and you lose as an employee and company. In the long run, this can hinder building a successful career or profitable company. For example, many big-box retailers in the past allowed customers to return any item with or without a receipt. However, they quickly found out it greatly detracted from their bottom line, because many customers took advantage of the policy with unethical practices.

Our Superstar Customer Service Edict is a win/win approach. As an employee, you are reminded that you are personally responsible and accountable for building customer loyalty with each customer you deal with. This means taking on the easygoing customers and the difficult ones one at a time. Customers win because each employee will focus on delivering the best service regardless of the situation. As a reminder for you, the Superstar service standards we discussed in Days 5–8 apply with every customer. After all, customers are always customers, regardless of their behavior.

## Who Is This *ss***e Customer?

Who knows for sure? We aren't psychologists that can psychoanalyze every difficult customer, and neither are you. We know them from experience working with more than a hundred companies worldwide, more than 200,000 managers, and more than a million employees. The impact of all of these organizations over the years has conservatively involved more than 5 billion customers. What we have learned is this: Some people or customers:

▶  Enjoy making situations toxic.

▶  Are mean, nasty, and rude.

▶  Have caustic personalities.

▶ Are very demanding and confrontational.

▶ Don't recognize or see themselves as a problem.

▶ Are the way they are because of a personality disorder, or another underlying issue or learned behavior and motivations.

▶ Are always difficult.

▶ Are difficult based on circumstances.

▶ Sometimes are our neighbors, friends, and family—really!

## How Do You Handle These Customers?

Always remember this adage: "You can't change other people. You can only choose and change how you respond to them." To preserve your principles and your sanity, consider these strategies to protect yourself with strength and power.

**All the Superstar standards apply**. Deal with any and all people with the utmost respect, dignity, and care, even if they don't seem to deserve it. Don't get into a shouting match and treat them poorly just because they are yelling out a diatribe. If you call them on their poor behavior they probably won't understand what you are talking about. Take responsibility for your part in the relationship.

**Make sure you start by listening.** Listening is the foundation of courtesy and respect. Tell them, "I want to help, sir. Tell me about it and let me take a few notes. Go ahead." It gives difficult customers the stage to air their grievances. In other words, let them vent. However, you have now directed the conversation so you are exerting positive influence.

**Try not to get defensive.** You need to work on building thick skin. Remind yourself that it's not about you; it's about them. This means whatever they are going through as a person, as well as the problem you need to help as a customer. They may attack you and accuse you of things you haven't done. By proxy, you are guilty for being part of the company you work for. You can learn to absorb it by learning to control your emotions through relaxation. Also, knowing your product, procedures, and options for solutions arms you with what you need to handle the situation. Always invest time in learning more about your role and company. It will serve you well when these difficult people come along.

**Then, deal with the person first, before you try to solve his or her problem.** He or she may blame you and yell at you and say unkind things. Acknowledge his or her difficulty. This means empathize and apologize.

For example, "I am so sorry this happened to you Mrs. X. I am sure this was an incredible inconvenience." Words from you expressed like this sincerely have a way of calming down even the most irate person.

**Be careful not to get angry.** If you get angry, you give the individual fuel to act out even more, while also justifying his or her case. You end up making an almost impossible situation worse. If you feel anger coming on, take a deep breath. Mentally, disassociate yourself from the situation by quickly reminding yourself of a pleasant memory, or use the Mental Psyche principles from Day 13 to refocus. Use the phrase *What I hear you saying is....* Or, apologize again. This gives you a little time to regroup your emotions. Finally, encourage yourself. Remind yourself that you are competent and confident, and have a commitment to doing the right thing. Remind yourself you are dealing with a customer and, no matter what, you want him or her to remain loyal to your company. Take this story:

> *In the past Rick had a job for a company that owned eight companies. Rick was the executive in charge of customer satisfaction and loyalty, and training. All departments had a poster for customers that directed them to his office if they didn't get satisfaction at their store. Once when Rick was in his office he received a call from an irate customer. The customer yelled, swore, and screamed at the top of his lungs how bad the service was he received yesterday, and that he would never, ever buy from the store again. He let all of his anger out on Rick. Finally, the customer took a breath. Rick genuinely replied, "I am so sorry you had that kind of experience in our store. I apologize that we, and I, let you down. However, I am delighted you contacted me. When good customers and people like you give us the feedback, we can find ways to be better. Thank you!" The customer gasped. Rick added, "Now may I ask a few questions to learn a few more specifics? I think I can help you." Rick kept him as a loyal customer.*

**Deal with the problem.** When the customer's anger slows or a breath is taken, recap the situation and his or her concern. Then, begin to focus on solutions. Tell the customer, "I am sad this has happened but I am happy you brought this to *my* attention. May I ask a few questions?... Here's what I can do...." Note that asking questions helps you navigate what really happened. Then, give the customer options. Demanding people like options because it gives them power to choose. By doing this you are leading the customer to an appropriate result and maintaining a chance to keep him or her as a customer.

**Use perspective questions to keep the customer honest and on track.** For example:

▶ "What I said was...."

▶ "That's not what I said."

▶ "What I can do is...."

▶ "Please let me finish."

▶ "I think we are saying the same thing."

Notice we are using "I" statements instead of "you" statements. If you say to the customer, "*You* didn't follow our policy," it comes across as an accusation. Instead, own the situation: "*I* believe this is a different circumstance than our policy. Let me share a few options."

**Remember: The secret to handling difficult, negative, and irate people is to manage yourself effectively.** Customers have freedom of speech, and they will express their views, whether right or wrong, because they can. With nearly 7 billion people in the world, you will have customers with contrary views. As you control your own emotional response and learn the techniques and skills discussed in the rest of the book, you will be well equipped to handle any situation professionally if not brilliantly.

---

**We Mentioned an Exception**

We believe our approaches work; they are time tested over the years with many employee, customers, and companies. However, some customers can be wacko. If a customer threatens you with violence and a verbal barrage, it's time to end the conversation and get help from your manager. You can end a conversation succinctly on the phone: "Mr. Customer, when you are ready to talk rationally I, or someone here, will help. I am ending the conversation now. Goodbye." Then report to your manager what happened and with whom. In person, say a similar statement and then go get help immediately. Don't risk your potential safety or your employees over a threat.

**Finally, know your company's approach.** Make sure you have conversations with your supervisor about these kinds of situations and what your policies and procedures are. We believe role-play and practice with voice and video recordings are great ways to learn how to deal with difficult situations effectively. You want to prepare so you can learn to get in "The Zone" when confronted by difficult people. "The Zone" is the place you go under pressure to perform your best without thinking. That's what Superstars do!

> *Customer satisfaction is worthless.*
> *Customer loyalty is priceless.*
>
> —Jeffrey Gitomer

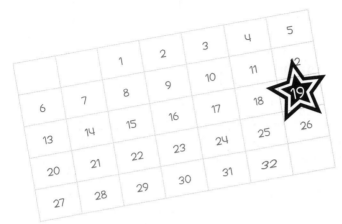

# How to Say NO! Hell No! (Nicely?)

It may seem like saying "no" is contrary to Superstar customer service. But it isn't. Sometimes you simply can't do what the customer wants. The following list gives the top 10 reasons to tell customers no:

1. It's against the law to do what they want.
2. It's unethical to do what they want.
3. It may cause harm to another person or you.
4. It may damage your company.
5. You don't have the product they want.
6. You don't deliver the service they want.
7. It's against your company policy.
8. You or your company isn't capable of doing what they want.
9. The customer is wrong or unreasonable.
10. The customer is lying.

Many times "no" adds fuel to the fire when customers are upset or complaining. Because of this, it is essential to learn how to say "no" in a way that maintains excellent customer service standards. Customers will get emotional if they feel they are losing control of the situation, being rejected, seen as being wrong, or facing conflict or opposition. To manage these feelings, here are seven guidelines for ensuring they keep their emotions in check and you keep them as a customer.

1.  **Give the customer alternatives to "no" while dealing with the customer with grace, dignity, and care.** How you say something is often more important than what you say—so important, in fact, that is can determine if the customer will ever come back. You need to be careful and ensure that saying no doesn't become a rule. A classic example comes from the movie *Miracle on 42nd St.* where a Macy's Santa Claus starts telling Macy's customers to go to Gimbels or other competitors when Macy's doesn't have the product, or the competition is better or cheaper. It becomes an advertising bonanza for Macy's with the goodwill it generates as employees tell customers, "We don't have that but let me recommend...." Similarly, at Disney World if a child isn't tall enough for a ride, they will give them a certificate for another ride. Cameron Mitchell Restaurants state that their culture suggests, "The answer is yes. Now what is the question."

    Learn and practice alternatives to saying "no." There are times that you can't do exactly what the customer wants. In these times the word *no* simply conveys a lack of willingness to try as it rejects the customer totally and leaves no opportunity for alternatives. Turn a negative into a positive, misery into magic, by saying "We aren't able to refund your money. What we can do is replace the product at no charge." or "We don't have that product in stock, but let me suggest the following..." or "This is a difficult situation and I apologize for the delay. I am glad to help. May I ask a few questions, so I can more effectively give you the best options?"

2.  **Remember: The customer may not always be right but the customer is still the customer**. *You* and your company need customers. Keep your mind focused on the fact that customers are top priority and you want to go out of your way to keep them. Don't look at them as inconveniences to your workday. You only have a workday because of their purchases.

3. **Be honest.** Don't mislead customers to think you will give them something you can't give. Say, "I really can't do that but what I can do is…," not "I doubt I can do that." Customers appreciate and respect honesty.

4. **Engage each customer individually.** A customer is a person, and his or her problem is special. Even though you may have to deal with similar problems all day long, treat each customer as an individual. Adjust to his or her style. With some you may need to be more direct, chatty, or analytical. By tuning into the person's style of communicating, you will be able to get on the same level right away and be able to solve problems faster.

5. **Be a good listener.** Listening involves 16 individual behaviors. Making eye contact, smiling, using verbal cues, thinking about how to answer, asking clarifying questions, and doing a listening check are just a few examples. If someone really listens to you, how to you feel? Important. That's how you want customers to feel when dealing with you.

6. **Always be polite and courteous, and avoid the following misery phrases that are essentially saying "no."** Sometimes the most costly mistakes can happen in only a few seconds upon making a customer contact on the phone or in person. These phrases create customer dissatisfaction. Here's also how to turn them into positive moments of truth or, as notable customer service speaker Shep Hyken says, "Moments of Magic."

   ▶ **Misery Phrase #1: "I don't know."**
   There is no need to ever utter these words. If you don't know, find out. Usually there isn't something you can't find out, outside of sensitive and financial information. Instead, create a positive moment of truth by saying, "That's an excellent question. Let me check and find out."

   ▶ **Misery Phrase #2: "We can't do that."**
   This one guarantees to upset your customers. You are supposed to help them, not shut them out. After all, they are paying the bill. Instead, respond by replying, "Boy, that's a tough one. Let's see what we can do." Then, find or brainstorm an alternative solution. You create positive moments of truth when customers know that you are on their side, trying to get things done on their behalf.

▶ **Misery Phrase #3: "You'll have to..."**
This sounds like an order or edict. As a rule, don't order customers around. They don't have to do anything they don't want to do except maybe pay taxes. Instead, use phrases such as:

➠ "A good next step is...."

➠ "Here's how we can help with that."

➠ "The next time this happens, here's what you can do."

➠ "May I suggest the following...."

▶ **Misery Phrase #4: "Hang on a second. I'll be right back."**
Most people fumble this one and leave the customer hanging. Instead, politely ask him or her to hold a minute or two. Be honest about the amount of time it will take and get back to the customer as soon as possible. For example, say, "It may take me two or three minutes to get that information. Are you able to hold while I check, or do you want me to call you back?" Or, "I need to do some research on that. How soon do you need the information? When I find the information, when is a good time to get back to you?"

▶ **Misery Phrase #5: "I understand."**
When you use this phrase what do you mean, really? If you haven't gotten to the root of the issue the customer will know that you don't really understand because he or she hasn't had a chance to explain. Instead, empathize genuinely by being a good listener, asking clarifying questions if needed, apologizing, and making a feeling statement. For example: "I know that you are frustrated with this process. I am sorry but I am here to help" or, "If that happened to me sir, I would be upset too. I apologize for your inconvenience. Let me help you, okay?" or, "I can tell you are very disappointed by what has happened. You have a right to be. I am so sorry. I want to help. May I ask a few questions to figure how best to do so?"

7. **Look for ways to over-deliver.** Why not add an exclamation point to your service? Think about how can you add value after helping someone. Remember you said "no" or used an alternative to say no. What support services does your company have that you can share with the customer (coupons, discounts, value pricing, comps, or added-on

products)? Sending a thank-you note or making a follow-up phone call to check in help to show the customer that you really care and will turn a situation where they were told "no" more enjoyable. Over-deliver without promising; surprise the customer.

You may have to say "no" many times in your career. With some courage and commitment and you can do it nicely with creativity, if not flair, without offending your customers or making them angry. In fact, if you do it correctly, you will often be able to establish a more loyal customer in the long run.

> *The single most important thing to*
> *remember about any enterprise is that there*
> *are no results inside its walls. The result of a*
> *business is a satisfied customer.*
> —Peter Drucker

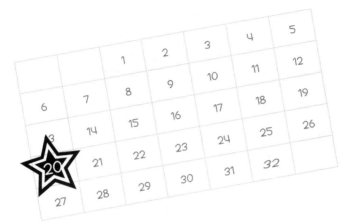

## How to Handle Complaints

As a customer, what do you expect when you find out that the product or service you paid for isn't good? Would you prefer:

1. Someone to listen to and understand your concern?

2. A knowledgeable and polite employee who is empowered to make a decision and do something?

3. Options to fix the problem?

4. A quick resolution, as immediate as possible?

5. An apology for your inconvenience or frustration?

6. A refund for your purchase?

7. Depending on the situation, some kind of compensation for your trouble?

8. Follow-through on what is agreed to and promised?

Too often when customers try to get complaints addressed, they come in contact with overworked and underappreciated employees. These employees will listen but most often can't make a decision and have to get a manager involved. Or, they are faced with the nightmarish task of finding how and where to file a complaint online. Often, they are put on hold or have to face an automated phone machine that can get frustratingly repetitive. Have you experienced any of this as a customer? How does this runaround make you feel? Does it increase your purchases and loyalty to that company's brand? Obviously not! Too many companies take their customers for granted, thinking they will always be there no matter the circumstance.

Most complaints can be handled satisfactorily. Most customers don't want to complain. Many are reasonable complainers. Our research shows that only one out of 20 people who could complain, do complain. That's five out of 100. Most customers are silent complainers who do this instead:

▶ Quit buying altogether at the company.

▶ Reduce their purchases and seek more pleasant alternatives.

▶ Tell all of their friends and family about their troubles. Now with social media options, any customer can reach millions of people through Facebook, Twitter, LinkedIn, and others in a heartbeat.

This is a real opportunity for any company and employee. For the company, this means they need to aggressively seek complaints by asking for customer feedback through surveys, market research, person-to-person interactions, and social media campaigns. The complaint you know about you can probably solve. It's the many complaints you don't know about that will hurt you.

## Your Role in Handling Complaints

In this day and age, we tell any person to be a student of the game. As we've mentioned, continuously learning about how to do your job better can only benefit you. Read the books, watch the DVDs or online programs, and attend seminars or webinars. Whether you have company support or not, you must Inc. yourself. No matter what job you have, you are ultimately in business for yourself. You don't do the job for free. In order to advance in your career and make your money, you have to excel. In your learning, keep finding ways to understand human behavior. We suggest the LAAF model as a way to handle 90 percent of the complaints you receive:

Listen

Apologize

Acknowledge

Fix

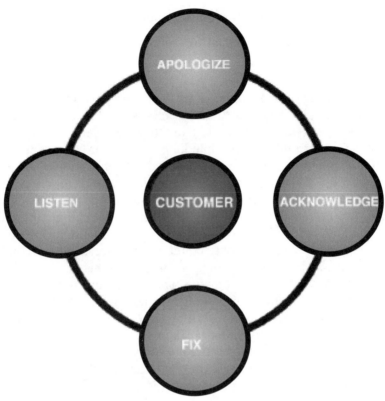

*Figure 20-1*

## Listen

Even though it may feel like all we do is listen to customers complain, this involves a very different type of listening. The LAAF model involves a type of active listening that requires not only attention, but intention—an intention to sincerely understand the customer's complaint, the trouble we have caused them by failing to meet or exceed their expectations, and how we can make things right. Effective listening will allow us to demonstrate the empathy and understanding that will show customers we genuinely care about them and how sorry we are for the mistake. Start by suggesting the customer tell you about their concern. Too many companies have employees start by asking for their name and account number. After you get the customer talking, wait for a pause or the end of the sentence to ask for the appropriate information. Excellent listening:

▶ Requires attention and intention.

▶ Requires a sincere intention to understand.

▶ Demonstrates empathy, understanding, and concern.

▶ Shows your customer that you care.

## Apologize

A key missing step in handling complaints is often simply to apologize sincerely. Often, it is tough for team members and team leaders to apologize to customers, because they are handling a complaint about something that "wasn't their fault." When handling a customer complaint, we must take full responsibility for the mistake, and deliver a sincere and genuine apology for the mistake. Again, this step will help us reinforce how much we appreciate the customer's business by demonstrating empathy and support. A very effective and easy way to do that is to maintain eye contact when handling complaints. For example, if there is a pricing complaint, a customer may come to the service counter and share his or her complaint. In many cases, while the customer is still sharing his dissatisfaction and frustration, we are often already working on the problem, processing a refund, and so forth, and may actually be making the problem worse: He may think he is being ignored. On the phone, set up a point of contact in your work area to focus on and make sure you use verbal phrases like "I see" or "Tell me more," or ask a question or two. An apology can be simply state such as this: "I am sorry that happened. I am sure it was frustrating. I apologize." When apologizing it is helpful to:

▶ Take responsibility for the mistake you probably didn't cause but you "own" because you work there.

▶ Deliver a sincere, genuine apology for the mistake or problem.

▶ Demonstrate empathy and support.

▶ Maintain eye contact, or, on the phone have a point of contact in your work area that you look at and use non-verbal cues.

## Acknowledge

As important as apologizing is to this process, acknowledging is equally as important. Acknowledging the complaint is important because it allows you take credit for being a good listener. It is important that we acknowledge the inconvenience we may have caused customers. For example, picture a mother who is shopping for her 7-year-old's birthday party with a house full of kids. She is at the store buying toys, gifts, and, of course, a birthday cake. After she gets home and her guests are getting ready to sing "Happy Birthday," she realizes she has left the candles on the bag carousel. This problem is much bigger than just getting her candles; she may feel like she has ruined the party. In this scenario, acknowledging that it was our mistake, even when it wasn't, will ease the customer's stress and make her appreciate that we are accountable and we are there for her.

- ▶ Acknowledge the inconvenience the problem may have caused.
- ▶ Acknowledge that it was our mistake and accept full responsibility.
- ▶ Be accountable.

### Fix

Lastly, once we have actively listened, apologized for the mistake, and acknowledged the inconvenience it may have caused, we must now find a friendly *fix!* Whenever a customer complains, you have two problems: how it affects the customer (frustration, anger, embarrassment, inconvenience) and the issue itself (poor quality, no follow-through, error, long lines). A friendly fix means you take care at each area. You see, you can give a refund, but if you don't deal with the customer's inconvenience you still have an unhappy customer. Few people with customer service responsibilities ever learn this, which is why the acknowledgment and apology steps are so important.

We must quickly take action, and provide an acceptable and agreeable solution for the customer. As we learned, if you are going to make a mistake, make it in favor of the customer. The "fix" itself is very important in responding to customer complaints. However, the steps leading up to the fix can dramatically impact how the customer feels about that experience. We can provide the best fix in the business, but if we don't take the time to actively listen, fully understand the inconvenience we've caused, take full responsibility, apologize, and then take appropriate action, we run the risk of fracturing that relationship and losing the customer. Remember these points:

- ▶ Find a friendly fix.
- ▶ Take action.
- ▶ Provide an acceptable, agreeable solution.
- ▶ Compensate the customer for the inconvenience.

To summarize, the LAAF model is an effective, easy-to-follow, step-by-step approach to dealing with customer complaints. This process allows us to effectively respond to the customer's need by demonstrating the empathy, understanding, and accountability necessary to effectively handle complaints. It also helps diffuse anger in particularly heated discussions with angry customers. And finally, it helps strengthen relationships with our customers in an effort to build a loyal customer base. The payoff for you is it makes your job easier and more enjoyable, because you can keep helping customers even when they are complaining. And you will feel good about how you do it because it works.

*The most important adage and the only*
*adage is, the customer comes first, whatever*
*the business, the customer comes first.*

—Kerry Stokes

# How Superstar Customer Service and Superstar Sales Go Together

We believe excellent selling is excellent customer service and vice versa. What is the general definition of service? It is meeting or exceeding your customers' needs and wants. What is the general definition of selling? It is meeting or exceeding your customers' needs and wants. Too often, fast-talking, sleazy salespeople give the honorable profession of sales a bad name.

Customer service and sales go hand in hand. In customer service, the goal is to focus on fulfilling the promise of your product or services. In sales, the goal is to offer new or existing customers your product and services. Everyone in the company, from the CEO to the new hire, is involved in customer service and sales. It's a competitive edge in any company if all customer contact employees are trained in customer service and sales skills. It also gives you as an individual a competitive edge if *you* understand the sales process.

We believe you can't really deliver Superstar customer service without knowing how to sell and actually do it as part of your customer service to customers. People become successful in a number of different ways in selling. One person may be particularly strong at presentations. Another may be most effective at building trusting relationships and fully understanding the customer's business needs and objectives. Research shows that effective salespeople excel in several key areas. Successful selling requires versatility, strong skills, and an unwavering commitment to customer-centered activity. Here are 10 core competencies and their definitions that will drive success in the sales world.

## 1. Customer-Centered Activity

Successful selling begins with the ability to approach the customer relationship with a complete focus on the customer—his or her business or personal needs, wants, and expectations. It also means doing business ethically to help customers achieve their goals, adapting your behavior to meet their style and focus of communication, relating effectively in terms of personal style, and reading their nonverbal communication. Flexibility and openness are crucial to testing your understanding of the customer's communication during the various stages of the buying process. When you are already serving the customer, a Superstar looks for ways to add value by helping the customer with additional needs and wants. So keep your eyes and ears open!

## 2. Effective Planning

Too many people fail at effectively planning. Be a student of the game and increase your ability to determine where you are in the relationship with the customer. Organize your workplace and day so you have all the tools you need to help. Know your customers. What are the typical types of customers you serve? What key products or services complement what existing customers are already using? Is your customer happy? What are the top 10 complaints, and how do you handle them? What are the advantages and disadvantages of your competition?

You must learn to prepare for your interactions so you can inquire about other needs or be ready to present other options for them. Of course, you always want to be of further service. The question is, how? Explore options through planning. Other areas of this competency include: personal organization, individual customer contact planning, company or department planning, coordination and teamwork with all internal and external resources.

## 3. Building Rapport with Customers

The truth is, everyone is selling something. It start with *you.* You had to sell yourself to get your job. You have to sell yourself in your relationships, particularly with your significant other. Building rapport is a process of gaining customers' trust so you help them. If you don't gain their confidence then they may look elsewhere for an associate they may deem more helpful.

So, how do you build rapport?

All excellent salespeople and customer service providers are masters at establishing rapport by creating a positive impression, dressing professionally, communicating clearly, listening effectively, asking good questions, using positive body language, and creating a safe and constructive communication climate with customers. In addition, you need to cast a wide net by building relationships with all key possible decision influencers, if it is appropriate for your situation. If you are in a call center taking calls for a credit card company this may not be necessary. If you are an IT professional helping install new software for a client, this consideration certainly applies.

## 4. Identifying Customer Needs

This core competency is about planning and executing a questioning strategy that enables you and the client to think through his or her personal or business needs. This will result in a clear and joint realization of the best product and service solution to address the customer's unmet and undefined needs. If your role is primarily engaging the customer and providing customer service to one degree or another, you want to pay attention to add-on products. This may include accessories, complementary items, or other services that will assist the customer based on what you have learned from him or her. This is even important for complaints that you handle well. Why not suggest: "I have an idea for you," "Have you ever thought about...?" "May I ask you an additional question?" or "How can I be of further assistance?" This involves thorough preparation, listening accurately, and raising client consciousness about unperceived needs or opportunities.

## 5. Presenting Solutions to Customers

Presentations to customers include developing solutions to client problems, developing effective benefit selling statements, and demonstrating new products and processes. This can be one short presentation or many longer presentations depending on your company's products and roles. Your style of delivery involves expressing yourself clearly, maintaining active dialogue in presentations, acting in a persuasive manner, presenting effectively to groups, using sales supports appropriately, and keeping technical presentations simple and understandable. It's all about learning to communicate clearly with influence, if not power. With practice through a speaking course or video playback, you can learn to be more effective. There is no substitute for ongoing practice, education, and training to improve your presentation skills.

## 6. Addressing Customer Concerns

Objections or problems stonewall many people in sales and customer service roles. Improve by asking for feedback on your proposed solution, expressing empathy for others, working with client resistance, dealing with interpersonal conflict, and repairing broken sales relationships. This competency also involves skilled application of the ability to create dialogue and mutual involvement during your customer contact. Most significantly, this involves skillfully working with the customer when he or she disagrees with your solution, or is angry or frustrated with you or your company. Remember the LAAF model we explored in Day 20 and apply that concept.

## 7. Closing the Sale

All sales activity is directed toward specific outcomes. This competency involves moving the customer to a commitment to use your products or services. Elements of the competency include "asking for the business," securing client commitments, and showing assertiveness and professionalism in negotiations. We coach and train others to do this simply as long as you have done the others steps well. Here are a few methods.

► **Action close:** "If I can get your approval right here, I'll have the order delivered promptly."

► **Alternative close:** "Do you what our Model A or Model B?"

► **Assumptive close:** "Which warranty do you want with your purchase? We have one-year, two-years, and four-years."

► **Added step close:** "Let's set a date for a follow-up meeting as a next step. What day is best next week?" or "If I can add value through marketing assistance to bring in more business, will you give me the opportunity to demonstrate our product?"

## 8. Follow-Up and Follow-Through

We call follow-up "The Greatest Closing Technique of All-Time." A few years after starting our consulting firm, our business slowed down. We did some homework and called nine key customers with ideas that could help them. We landed seven new contracts. It taught us a valuable lesson about following up. For those of you who aren't salespeople, follow-up means regular or added value phone and e-mail contact with customers. For employees who deliver products to customers, this includes paying attention to their needs and sharing with customers other ways you can help. For service technician roles where you go on-site to fix customer products or do warranty maintenance, it means learning customers' needs better and seeking other way to better serve them. All customer contact personnel must generate appropriate written correspondence to customers, act on expected action steps, coordinate activity and outcomes within your company, and keep adequate records to increase penetration in existing accounts. As a guideline, think about what everyone else does in your role. How can you distinguish yourself? What added touch can you provide? That's Superstar customer service.

## 9. Leveraging Team and Organizational Support

Today you need to function as an external and internal team member, and be able to relate effectively to all support personnel in your company. Smooth transitions from one department to the next and speed to action in critical situations often become differentiators in the customer's eyes. Teamwork is a must. You need to ensure that information and activity flow in support of customer commitments, and expectations are communicated and completed consistently to others you work with. Team players are good listeners, supportive, helpful, and understanding. When mistakes are made they don't play the blame game. Instead, they ask, "How can we fix this together?" Team players treat their coworkers as good as or better than the external customer.

## 10. Emotional Resiliency and Peak Performance

Working with customers is demanding. Dealing with complaints and handling rejection add to the stress of the job. A key ingredient to sustainable success for your role is to maintain appropriate life balance. To deliver Superstar customer service consistently, you need to learn to become emotionally resilient in order to achieve your peak performance.

There are two kinds of stress: *distress,* which is negative stress, and *eustress,* which is positive stress. Stress comes from the events in our lives. How we perceive these events at any given point determines if there is a negative or positive impact. Humans do require a degree of stress to survive. Think of stress as a balloon. Without the air, a balloon is not much use or fun. With the right amount of air it can be enjoyable and fulfill its purpose. With too much air, it pops!

Distress comes from too many negatively perceived stressful events in life: life changes, financial issues, sickness, relationship difficulties, family concerns, fatigue, job problems, and so on. If too many of these situations happen at once or during an extended period of time, you get stress overload.

We can learn to alleviate the distress by engaging in more activities that give you positive feelings and fulfillment. Examples include reading, sporting events, hobbies, exercise, a healthy diet, education, relaxation activities, accomplishing a goal, personal recognition, relationships with loved ones, and career progress or success. The point is this: Take care of yourself and you will be better able to take care of the customer.

Be open to analyzing your performance. Review your progress on your work goal plans regularly. Continuously focus on learning and developing your ongoing effectiveness. This means your work and life balance as well.

To summarize, the consistently outstanding performer in dealing with the customer knows how to sell. These 10 competency areas give you a way to benchmark your capability. You don't simply master one and then take it for granted. You keep polishing your skills and expanding your knowledge. As the old adage goes, "Life is a journey, not a destination." So continued excellence is a process of periodically taking inventory of your strengths and opportunities for improvement and doing something about them. Finally, remember this quote for career success: "We are what we repeatedly do; excellence is not an act but a habit."

If you are looking for a more detailed analysis of Superstar selling check out our book *Superstar Selling: A 31-Day Plan to Motivate People, Build Rapport, and Close More Sales* on our Website (*www.wcwpublishing. com*).

> *Quality in a service or product is not what*
> *you put into it. It is what the client or*
> *customer gets out of it.*
>
> —Peter Drucker

## Working With the Numbers
### Let's Get Real—You Are Going to Be Measured!

As business evolves and competition heats up more and more emphasis is placed on the measurement of results. For the past 35 years, there has been a constant search for tools to measure performance and hold employees accountable for their efforts on the job. It has been said that "what gets measured, gets done." Though this is not always true, the reality is that the search goes on. It doesn't matter what business you're in or what job you hold, the organization is and will be measuring sales and expenses and profitability, and they will look for ways to both measure productivity and to continuously increase it. This means that the measurement will extend down to the specifics of what you do in your job on a day-to-day basis. So, you want to know:

1.  **What success looks like.** What are the success metrics that the leaders of your business pay attention to? This gives you tremendous insight into how the business is being operated, and what areas of focus you can pay attention to and learn about in order to advance your career.

2.  **Exactly how you're being measured both functionally and personally.** Early on, it will give you insight into what aspects of the job are most important to your boss and the company. It also gives you some idea on how your performance can help you to be promotable on the job.

Let us warn you: The hard stuff is almost always the part that involves interacting with customers. The tendency for most people with a customer service role is to emphasize the technical aspects of the job. However, assuming that doing a good job functionally will take care of the most important aspects of your customer service role can be detrimental.

Doctors assume that their ability to "practice good medicine" is absolutely the most important thing for them to do, thinking, "If I can treat and heal the disease, I've done my job." Pharmacists have a strong tendency to believe that turning out prescriptions accurately and in a timely manner is what is most important to their patients. Computer specialists and technical support personnel usually see the most important part of their job centered on the proper setup of the hardware and the ability to find the software/operating system conflicts and correct them. In the restaurant and retail worlds, the focus is on getting the food in front of the customer or the retail products on the shelves with a presentable appearance. However, the thing that gets shortchanged in all of these scenarios is the customer. By that, we mean many things. For example, how is the customer affected by the illness, or what problems or concerns is the customer having with his medications or the side effects she may be experiencing from the medication? What questions does the customer have about how to use the product or which version may be best for his or her needs and budget? These human dynamics are present in every job where there is a customer on the other end. They are the most difficult aspects of the job, and they are the element that is most unpredictable and messy. Get it right and you can become a Superstar.

To do this successfully, you must learn how to anticipate and deal with issues that arise. When you do, you'll be invaluable to the business. If you are the one whose name frequently comes up on guest feedback surveys as the one who helped and got it right, you win credibility and will be valued by your employer. However, if that is not you, and if you are the one who is a brilliant technician but who can't get it right with the customers, you will achieve your highest level of organizational worth early in your career. If you excel at one aspect of your job, but minimize the importance of another, your overall impact will be less than stellar.

We have consulted with a nuclear power company for more than 15 years now on the development of their leadership talent. We work with middle- and upper-level managers in the organization, so we get a chance to see and coach many individuals as they work their way up the organization's chain of command. It is very gratifying to play a small part in the development of these individuals through the course of their careers; as you might imagine, during 15 years we have seen a lot of movement through the organization. One frustrated individual said, "I came from a family that put tremendous value on education. I studied hard and got excellent grades all of the way through my schooling from grade school, through high school, through college, and up to and including my schooling as an engineer. I went to the best private schools available to me and when I went on to university, I went to a fine Ivy League school. Now, after I've worked for a number of years in my career I can see a pattern developing that disturbs me a great deal." We listened to him as he built the framework around his point of view, and we held up our end of the conversation until he finally made his point. With a pained expression he said, "All of this time I put all of my attention on being the smartest and best student, employee, engineer, etc., and now it's clear to me that the people who are moving up in the organization are the ones who got C's in school, but learned how to interact with and get along with people." This was not good news to him, and typically it isn't to too many other professionals either. Being the smartest person in the room or in the organization is valuable only in as much as you can interact with, empathize with, understand, engage, influence, and help the person or people around you. If you have both great intellect and great people skills—often referred to as emotional intelligence—you have the potential to be a Superstar.

One of the topics we discussed in Day 7 includes a balanced look at the skills and capabilities each Superstar customer service provider needs to possess and utilize skillfully on a day-to-day basis. "Balanced" in this case refers to the importance of basic technical capabilities relevant to your business, balanced with fundamental interpersonal relationship management skills, and the ability to marry the two in many roles so that you can help people through the difficulties of their frustrations and many complex technical and business issues simultaneously. Together, these bundles of dynamic, ever-changing problems are what make most jobs truly difficult and challenging.

We've often heard clients say some variation of "Things would be great if we didn't have to deal with the customers." It's true: Customers can be maddening, challenging, heartbreaking, and just all around difficult to deal with. For teachers, it's the difficulty of getting through to a student. It's not just mastering the material and being able to present it. To the service technician, it's how to diagnose a difficult breakdown in a customer's car, and how to work with a customer who can't afford to be without his product and is unsure if he can trust you to fix the problem correctly without running up large, unnecessary bills that he has to pay. At the same time, you have a line of people with similar issues right behind this customer. All are experiencing some variation on the same themes and it is only 7:45 a.m. in your upcoming 12-hour shift. Welcome to the world of customer service.

These days you can bet that your company is collecting data to measure your performance and the performance of the whole company through the eyes of your customers. Most businesses regularly collect survey information at the point of sale or as an immediate post-sales interaction. Many also engage a firm to "mystery shop" their different customer contact points. These two tools may together generate tens of thousands of survey responses during the course of a month, and you can bet that customers are allowed and encouraged to provide direct comments via their recorded telephone calls or through paper and pencil surveys, or most likely via the Internet. The mystery shop is based on a trained individual coming into your place of business as a customer would and engaging the business and employees in the same kinds of transactions that your customers experience daily. Mystery shop professionals are looking for specific kinds of interactions and transactional elements that have been deemed important to the way you choose to do business. For example, did the health professional wash his or her hands upon entering the examination room, before engaging in your checkup?

They measure multiple things including: OSAT (Overall Customer Satisfaction); whether you would refer a friend or family member to this business based on your experience; whether you were greeted; and whether the provider wore a name tag and/or introduced him- or herself. The list goes on and is tailored to the specifics of your business. The key message here is you need to know the answers to these questions sooner rather than later. Use this knowledge to guide your learning, your practice, and your performance on the job.

As a result, business leaders can see patterns and trends in the way we, as customer service providers, conduct ourselves with our customers on a day-to-day basis. This data, combined with the day-to-day observations of your supervisor and/or manager, give a fairly clear snapshot of who is a Superstar and who is simply "going through the motions." If you deceive yourself into thinking that you're the best because you went to the best schools and got the best grades and that you're the smartest one on your team, guess what? You're wrong. Remember: It's just as likely that our engineer was the one who really has it figured out. You're better off to be at least "middle of the pack" smart—and also to be brilliant when it comes to working with and interacting with the customer. If you listen for understanding, ask good questions, empathize, repeat back what you understand, solve the problem with the customer, and make and keep promises repeatedly, your name will show up on surveys as the one who customers love to work with. Be the one who your customers count on. They will come back time and again, and wish everyone treated them so well. You can become a legend at your company, and your job will take you as far as you are willing to go. A true Superstar!

| Superstar Customer Service Application |
|---|
| 1. What are the highest priority performance areas for your work group? |
| 2. What are the aspects of your group's performance that your manager or supervisor tracks to know how well the group is performing? |
| 3. What are the key aspects of your job that you must do well in order to perform effectively, overall? |
| 4. Most jobs involve a more technical aspect of responsibility and a customer impact element within the job. Highlight or describe the elements of each. |
| Technical aspects: |
| Customer engagement aspects: |

| **Superstar Customer Service Application (continued)** |
|---|
| 5. Identify one or two areas where you can improve your performance in order to become a well-rounded Superstar. |
| 6. Describe your plan to practice and improve your performance in each. |

You want to know how to play the game. What does success look like? How will your manager be evaluating your performance? What is the business trying to accomplish with and for its customers? Remember: Performance includes the way this organization wants to be seen in its marketplace. It includes everything from how we meet and interact with the public to our appearance, uniform, and so forth.

> *Don't lower your expectations to meet your performance. Raise your level of performance to meet your expectations. Expect the best of yourself, and then do what is necessary to make it a reality.*
>
> —Ralph Marston

## Surveys, Mystery Shop, Complaints, and Written Notes

At first, when people are learning something new, many prefer not to keep score. After being first introduced to tennis years ago, we would take some old, lifeless tennis balls to a tennis court and volley, back and forth, for hours. One of us had played tennis before, but the sport was completely new to the other. We were challenged at first by hitting the ball, then by controlling our shots so that they stayed in the court. Then, it was learning to place our shots inside the singles boundaries. Finally, it was learning other strokes (the backhand, the serve, etc.) that would help our overall game. Each aspect was interesting and appealing in its own way. There was no criticism and feedback was minimal—except for the feedback received from hitting the ball and watching the outcome.

We learned the basic rules of the game as they seemed relevant. For example, you get two attempts to serve from behind the service line into the opponent's service box. If you hit the net with your serve, you must try again, even if the ball goes into the service box. Back and forth, we hit the ball, all the while enjoying the motion and "getting the feel" for the equipment and learning a bit more about the rules. Later in the day, a more experienced tennis player came to the court without a partner and patiently watched us while waiting to get on the court. As we surrendered the court to him he asked us if we would like to hit the ball with him. He had newer, better tennis balls, and was patient with our beginner skills and minimal understanding of the game. He offered some compliments when either of us made a good shot or tried hard to get to a difficultly placed ball. He also made a few suggestions on technique or how to cover the court. After a while, he suggested we play a game and guided us through the scoring system. Soon the game began to take on the life of competition. Before long, we were using the language of tennis, scoring our games, and keeping track of sets won and lost. Though we still enjoy warming up and practicing ground strokes before the game begins, as soon as we got a basic understanding of how you keep score and how you play the game, tennis took on a whole different meaning. The fun multiplied as we refined our game and played with other tennis players. We began to learn more about strategy, shot placement, and how and when to move to the net. Now we have the tools to compare our game with our past performance. We can tell much more about the quality of our play and our competiveness against other players, and we can zero in on certain skills that help us be competitive or, on the other hand, that make us vulnerable to other players.

Almost all popular sports have their own scoring systems. They are generally understood by all of the players and coaches, and the rules stay the same from game to game and from team to team. The same is true when it comes to measuring our performance as customer service providers. In fact, many of rules of customer service translate from one business to another.

Overall customer satisfaction is a measure of the "total customer experience." *How did we do at satisfying your needs across all of the things that matter to you in your engagement with this business? Based on your experience, would you refer a friend to this business?* As businesses become more sophisticated at working with their customers, they learn more about the things that really matter to them. They find ways to measure them, and as the measures become more reliable and representative of the customers' experience, they also become more valuable as a mechanism to track and improve performance within the business. As a customer service provider, whether you are in retail, are in distribution, or provide a service, a major element of your competitiveness in your marketplace is centered around the impact you make on your customers. Most companies set up their own feedback monitoring systems and track their own service to enable them to use the feedback as guidance for continuous improvement. Point-of-sale survey systems are becoming increasingly common. For example, airlines sample customers on various aspects of their flight experience after almost every trip. This information is analyzed and used to guide further improvement in the airline's performance with a goal of winning their customers' hearts and minds so that they become loyal customers who will come back again and again when they have a reason to fly or use any other service.

It is beneficial to pay attention to measures taken by your company. Service numbers collected are often designed to measure trends in areas of customer performance. Measures taken on individual elements of the service process, as well as seeking a measure on overall performance, are used to determine "how we're doing" as an organization. If you pay attention to the numbers your organization is tracking, it will give you a great deal of insight into the specific kinds of behaviors your leaders are asking for and expecting from you and your colleagues. You can use that information to better understand the playing field you're working in and the specific performance that your organization values. Most of the measures that come in will represent behavior or performance by your organization as a whole, or by specific functions within the service chain. Use this knowledge to monitor your skill and priorities, and determine if there is an opportunity for you to add value to your performance by improving your skill in some aspect of customer engagement. It may be a matter of behavioral emphasis, or it may require training and skill practice for you to improve. The point is that the awareness of the "rules of the game" will give you guidance in those areas of performance the leadership of your organization values and seeks to develop within the organization's workforce.

Feedback from each of the collection methods yields different types of results, and some of it may be more pointed and personal. Many surveys provide the opportunity for customers to make comments that are recorded and fed back verbatim within the survey reports. In those cases, it is possible that you may receive comments that include your name and, report on a particular customer's response to a service you provided. Hopefully, the comment will report a positive experience as a result of your involvement. If not, it is important not to panic and get defensive about the feedback. Sometimes you hit your serve outside of the service box, and sometimes you hit the ball into the net. Neither of these outcomes fits with what was intended, but the result of your action is yours alone. You are the one who can improve or fix the performance problem. Your goal should be to learn from any feedback you receive, whether it is personal and directed at your performance alone, or whether it is cumulative and represents an amalgam of many sets of perceptions about many individual performers within the organization. If you remain non-defensive, learn from the feedback, and use it to guide your personal feedback, your customers and the leadership in your organization will notice your efforts. Your improved performance and overall constructive attitude will often result in positive performance ratings and even promotion within your organization.

Organizations are always interested in employees who take an interest in the business, develop their own capability to add value continuously, and help the business accomplish its objectives by generating positive customer experience. This is the mark of a customer service Superstar.

| Superstar Application |
|---|
| 1. Identify the key measures that your manager and your manager's manager refer to and report on consistently over time. This may be a "dashboard" that consolidates a series of specific measures on a regular basis and that provides comparisons to past measures of the same performance areas. |
| 2. Based on reporting from these areas of measurement, what performance areas are most important to your organization? |

| **Superstar Application** (continued) |
| --- |
| 3. Using those measures as a gauge of overall and individual performance importance, how do your skills and past performance "stack up"? In other words, which of these things have you done well historically, and where are their opportunities for you to improve? |
| 4. Have you received any personal feedback from customer surveys or supervisory observation that specifically mentioned performance strengths or opportunities to improve? If so, what are they? |
| 5. Find somebody else who is particularly skilled at any area that you can benefit from improving. Look for opportunities to watch him or her in action or ask for guidance and feedback. |
| 6. If your organization values management coaching, ask your supervisor to give you a few tips and provide coaching for improvement when opportunities arrive. |

Your self-directed search for improvement will pay dividends, as you become a true customer service Superstar.

> *Your most unhappy customers are your*
> *greatest source of learning.*
>
> —Bill Gates

## You Are Going to Hear About It, So You May as Well Make It Work for You, Not Against You

Just what are you going to hear about?

Well, if you're lucky, you'll get clear communication and information about what is expected of you in your job, and how to do it. However, there are no guarantees.

You're probably going to hear about it when you do something that upsets a customer, a coworker, or a supervisor. These messages may be heated, direct, or loud and clear. Adversely, they may be indirect, obtuse, even veiled. Or, they may be cold, formal, and impersonal.

You're going to hear about it when you make any mistake that someone thinks is serious. Hopefully it will be delivered in a constructive and helpful manner. It may, on the other hand, be delivered via a threatening look or an impersonal e-mail or memo.

You may hear about it when you do a good job or when you go above and beyond the regular expectations of your job.

### Become Personally Responsible for Your Own Excellence

From years of working with executives, managers, and supervisors, we know there is no guarantee that you're going to be the recipient of competent communication, good training, regular feedback, and coaching. In most organizations, the idea of praising good performance, and recognizing contributions and accomplishment, is almost unheard of. After all, you were hired to do a good job, weren't you? The situation isn't usually serious but you are probably going to have to do a fair amount of self-training and independent problem-solving. Your ability to watch, learn, and listen for unspoken expectations will be an invaluable skill as you work hard to rise above the difficulties that are present in every job and every organization. Yes, somebody should have trained you. And, they should have told you how to handle that situation that you're now facing. And, yes—right now you're facing a real live customer without that knowledge or skill development. As a Superstar, you will succeed or fail based on your own ability to make it work. And, you'll learn how to handle it better next time.

So, heads up, pay attention, observe, and listen for what's being said and what's not. Ask questions, bring your common sense with you, and learn, learn, learn, practice, practice practice. It doesn't matter if your job is working at the counter at a fast food restaurant, fielding 911 callers or working the emergency room triage center at a major hospital; each requires a person who is willing to manage his or her own attention and focus, work hard, bring good judgment, and get better day-by-day. Remember: We're looking for Superstar performance, the kind of performance that makes you stand out above the rest.

## Practice and Work to Discover Excellence

Excellence usually presents itself as an experience, not just knowledge. Knowing how to do something and being able to do something are two very different things. Just because you know how to do something, it doesn't mean you can do it. In many circumstances, the cliché "it's much easier said than done" holds true. Delivering excellence in customer service is difficult, challenging, and in most cases, very hard to master.

When you hit a baseball just right—in the sweet spot—you feel almost no stinging vibration through the bat and into your wrists, shoulders, and hands. It feels good. The ball leaves the bat like a rocket, and travels very far effortlessly. However, if you swing hard, hit it, but don't connect perfectly, the impact can send a vibration through the bat that stings your hands and causes pain through your wrists, shoulders, and sometimes right up to your jawbone.

Unless you experience that "solid hit," you will never really exactly understand the feeling of a perfectly hit baseball. After you've played the game and practiced long enough to get yourself in shape physically, and you've swung at and hit enough baseballs, you'll experience the "feel" of a well hit ball often enough to recognize it and appreciate it. You'll also find that it happens more frequently. It will become less of an accidental, unexplainable occurrence, and a more predictable outcome of your practiced eye on the ball, skilled timing, and well-controlled swing. When all of these things come together and you meet the ball solidly—crack—the ball travels as if it has wings and a life of its own. You recognize and appreciate that excellence. That feeling of near perfection brings you back and motivates you to do it again.

The truth is, even professional athletes don't hit the "sweet spot" every time they try. There may be long periods of time when it seems like they can't find the sweet spot. Even though they practice, they still make small mistakes, and swing too hard or not hard enough. We all know how to swing a bat; it's not rocket science, but it takes training and perseverance to hit it well. Though you may not get it the first time, you can get better. You can practice and improve your conditioning and, through time, achieve a new level of skill and readiness. The same is true for your job as a customer service provider. It looks simple in many cases. However, there is a huge difference between those who know how to find the sweet spot, anticipate needs, and be ready, responsive, and adaptable, and those of us who simply talk a good game.

## What Are You Listening For?

Listen for the messages about what is important and what is valued. Some of the messages are embedded in the organization and its core value system. Some of these expectations exist and are communicated in the clichés, slogans, and frequent quotes from founders or individuals who have achieved legendary status in the organization. Some are clearly stated; others are difficult to hear clearly or at all.

## Don't Be "Tone Deaf"

It is important not to ignore or minimize the wrong message. In many workplaces, its consequences can be not only job threatening, but deadly. For example, our long-time, highly valued nuclear power client holds safety above everything else. There isn't a meeting or training session that doesn't begin with the proper safety information and directives: escape and exit routes, what to do if confronted with an emergency, locations of safety equipment, and a heads-up on risky situations that may be confronted are communicated. Every employee is both empowered and expected to caution any other employee, including senior leadership. When they are doing something that carries a safety risk, any employee can stop work and call a "stand down" when they are unsure how to proceed or perceive an unsafe situation. For this reason it is important for their employees to never be tone deaf when it comes to listening to the safety messages in this organization. If they were ignored or minimized by any employee, the consequences could be dire.

After working in more than one organization you may be surprised that they don't do things the same way as they did at your last job. Some expectations may be hardwired in and carry significant rewards or punishment. You cannot afford to be blinded by your past experiences and risk missing these expectations. Listen carefully for your new workplace's messages and, if you're not hearing them, ask your boss and or colleagues, "What are the absolutes here?" "What are the things that we always do?" "What are the things that we never do?" "What do people get promoted for in the job that we do?", and "What do people risk getting fired for in the job that we do?" In addition to this, watch and study performance reports and feedback, listen to your manager, and observe what is rewarded, what is seen as a problem, or what is unacceptable. These messages are extremely informative and will help guide your development. Gathered together and constantly monitored, they hold the potential to guide you to excellence and Superstardom.

## Feedback Is Everywhere

Traditional avenues such as surveys, mystery shops, and performance reports give you great insight into what the company values. Social media sites such as blogs, Facebook, Twitter, and StumbleUpon provide a less traditional, structured source of feedback that can fill in additional gaps. Contributors speak to what they think is important; political correctness and the fear of offending someone in power simply are not concerns or filters for ratings and comments. Yelp, founded in 2004, collects feedback and comments on thousands of professions and businesses worldwide, and to date has received more than 39 million reviews from consumers. Users select an overall rating and make comments about their experience. These comments can be very informative regarding the expectations and experiences of the customers of your business or service. Here is one example, a review for a local hardware store:

> *[It] is literally around the corner from my awesome-but-needs-a-lot-of-work apartment. We've been in and out of here almost 2 or 3 times a week for every manner of house maintenance issue: plumbing, painting, making keys, gardening, electrical, hardware. Seriously, everything. Every time we come in we're greeted (with a 'Welcome*

*back!' most times) and they have a super well trained knowledgeable staff who are able to answer questions and direct you to your desired items. They really blew us away this last week when they proceeded to walk us around the store (to almost every department) to point out the item that we asked to find. They're just about the friendliest, most helpful hardware employees I've met. When they can't get something for you (they didn't have the blank for one of the keys we needed copied) they'll point you in the right direction. Yes, you'll be paying (a little, not a lot) more than you might at the depot. But the convenience and the service are well worth it."*

This brief description of this customer's experience at this small hardware store reveals a lot of information that may not appear in a survey or mystery shop. As an aspiring Superstar, you can gain a lot of insight into how to create a special experience for your customers if you work in this store or one similar.

## Creating Excellence—One More Time

Focusing on excellence is not easy, but it's worth it. A colleague in the training and development business used to say, "I'll take try," which can be understood to mean, "I'd rather have someone who is willing to try to improve, to try learn something, to try to get better, than someone who has decided that they already know it." "You can't teach me anything" usually translates into "I'm not willing to learn anything." Along with that decision often comes the perception that there are always good reasons why the customer was the problem: "Nobody could make that grumbler happy."

So, keep coming back, keep trying, get more coaching and guidance, and review your feedback. Listen, even when it's hard and frustrating. Avoid the temptation to take the easy way out, quit, or settle for mediocre performance. Avoid blaming the conditions, your coworkers, and the customers themselves. You have the opportunity to shape your own capability and contribution, and, with that, you will benefit. Maybe it will happen here, in this job, or maybe in the next one. Companies are always looking for the true professionals. Excellence always stands out; it's noticeable and will be found even if you aren't quite sure of something. We'll take "try." So, try! You can be great and you're worth it. You're a Superstar!

> *It is not the employer who pays the wages.*
> *Employers only handle the money. It is the*
> *customer who pays the wages.*
> —Henry Ford

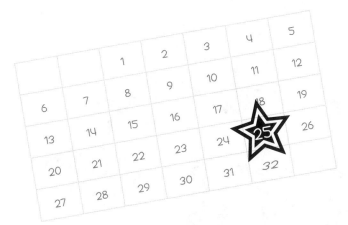

## Follow-Up Strategies and Going the Extra Mile

It is clear by now that you can separate yourself from the pack by the choices you make to be a Superstar in your customer service environment. Managing yourself and your perception of your role gives you a chance to stand out in your customer's service experience.

In this chapter, we want to focus on two separate, but interrelated strategies: first, follow-up strategies, and second, going the extra mile.

The opportunity to serve is rooted in the reality that the customers you serve are here because they have a need. It may be a problem, like when something is broken (consultant or repair person) or they are in some sort of pain (health-related issue or need for counsel or guidance). Perhaps they need a tool or a resource to help them fulfill some other need or expectation (real estate or lodging for the night).

In Day 20, we discussed the use of the LAAF model to help when customers are upset or have a problem. To recap, LAAF is a process model (behavioral guide) for customer service providers to use when dealing with customers who have a complaint or objection about prices, products, or services. Customers complain or get upset for many reasons. Sometimes they can't find what they want or it's too expensive; sometimes they're just having a bad day. LAAF is a simple but effective way to handle those problems: listen, apologize, acknowledge, and fix.

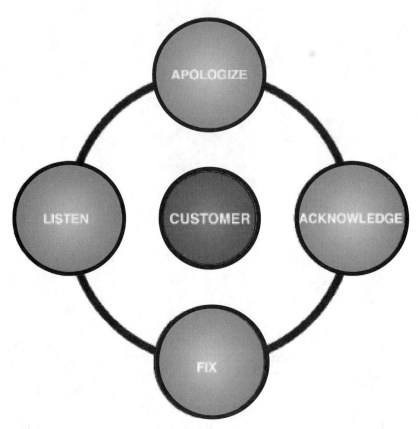

*Figure 25-1*

**Listen.**         This refers to "active listening" that requires not only
                    attention, but also *intention.* It demands intention to
                    sincerely understand the customer's complaint, the trouble
                    we have caused the customer by failing to meet or exceed
                    his or her expectations, and how we can make good.

**Apologize.**      We must take full responsibility for the mistake and
                    deliver a sincere and genuine apology for the mistake—
                    even though we personally may not have been the one
                    who made the mistake.

**Acknowledge.** It is important that we acknowledge the inconvenience we
                    may have caused the customer. Take responsibility for it
                    and be accountable for it.

**Fix.**            Take action. Provide an acceptable, agreeable solution
                    that compensates the customer for the inconvenience.

## Follow-Up Activities

Follow-up is an important way to bring closure to an issue and get back into the customer's good graces. It demonstrates to the customer that you really do care about him or her and that your apology was more than just a way to get out from under the discomfort of the customer's complaint or dissatisfaction—while also giving you an opportunity to personalize your concern and demonstrate your sincerity because, after all, you remembered him or her and you cared enough to ensure that the problem was resolved. Follow-up may take the form of a phone call in response to a comment the customer left on a survey or it may be that you made it a point to get the customer's phone number so you could "stay with him or her" and make sure the problem was solved. It may be that you send an e-mail or even visit the customer personally to follow up and communicate your concern, your well wishes, and your intention to "make it right." This is not common, everyday service activity; if you do it regularly and work hard at it, you will stand out from the pack.

## Going the Extra Mile

*It's never crowded along the extra mile.*

—Wayne Dyer

In the book of Matthew, Jesus teaches his disciples the principles of humility and a "servant heart" when he says, "Whoever compels you to go one mile, go with him two." It is more than giving extra effort; it is a call to do acts of service with the right attitude.

Going the extra mile calls on you to be prepared to do the unusual or extraordinary. It often involves hearing that "little voice" in your head that says, "You should...." Often what the little voice suggests is not comfortable and not part of the regular job or even normal behavior. It's like when that little voice says, "You should pick up the check for that elderly couple," or "You should pay for the ice cream cones for that young family who may not be as well off as you." It may say, "You should hold open that door or carry the baggage for that businessperson who seems stressed and over-burdened." It is called the extra mile precisely because it's always more than is expected and often an extra burden to take on.

There are at least three elements to going the extra mile. You need to:

1. Look for opportunities to help.
2. Have an attitude that says, "It's my business to help."
3. Listen to the little voice that says, "You should..." and go ahead and do it. Make it your business to help.

Take action! Don't pass up an opportunity to do something extraordinary. Also, follow up and follow through. Once you're involved, stay with the customer until you're sure his or her need is handled or problem is fixed.

In October 2012, Ben Baltz ran in Florida's Sea Turtle Tri Kids triathlon. Ben had lost his right leg to bone cancer when he was 6, having his fibula and tibia removed. He uses a mechanical knee and prosthetic leg to help him walk, run, and do other physical activities. During this event, Ben had swum 150 yards, had biked 4 miles, and was halfway through the 1-mile run when a screw came loose in his prosthetic leg and his running leg broke in half.

Kim Baltz, Ben's mother, was waiting at the finish line wondering why Ben hadn't finished yet. She knew he was nearly finished with the race, and it seemed like it was taking him way to long to come into view and finish. Before her worries became too burdensome, she heard the announcer tell the crowd to turn so they could see what was happening on the course.

She and the other audience members spotted Ben with Matthew Morgan, Private First Class at Marine Detachment Corry Station, who had noticed Ben's broken prosthetic leg, and carried him on his back for the remainder of the 1-mile stretch. They were accompanied by his fellow Marines. The story and pictures taken by CNN iReporter Ben Kruggel have been viewed on the web by thousands of viewers.[1] Many people were in tears to see the group of young Marines proudly help young Ben complete his triathlon. This is going the extra mile.

We have experienced many people during our careers who have gone the extra mile for us. We've had help from individuals who walked us around a big-box home improvement store to help us find exactly what we needed and explained how to use each element of our repair job. We've sat in restaurants where waiters or waitresses diplomatically steered us away from menu selections that they thought might not meet our expectations. In a small town in Italy a helpful gentleman who didn't speak English took time from his schedule and used his personal automobile to drive us to a location we were unable to locate. Once we had arrived, he absolutely refused our attempt to reimburse him for his time and expense.

Sometimes going the extra mile means listening to an upset or distraught individual. Sometimes it involves doing something to make a chore or difficult task go easier or to relieve the frustration someone is experiencing. We know for certain that if you make it your practice to always bring your best and consistently look for opportunities to go the extra mile, you will distinguish yourself from the average, everyday efforts and attitudes we all experience as we interact with business and service providers day-to-day.

| Superstar Application |
|---|
| 1. Recall one or two times that you have gone the extra mile to help someone in your business. |
| 2. What prompted you to go beyond regular expectations, to go the extra mile? |
| 3. Did you second-guess yourself after you were "out there"? |

| **Superstar Application (continued)** |
|---|
| 4. Describe the outcome and or reaction of the individual(s) you reached out to help. |
| 5. Did anybody else notice what you had done? If so, how did they react to your effort and commitment? |
| 6. How did you feel as a result of your effort? |

*Always do more than is required of you.*
—George Patton, former general,
United States Army

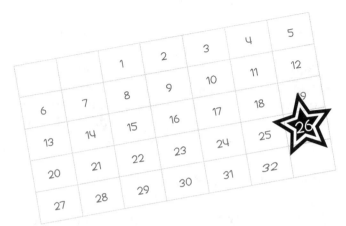

# What to Do When Things Go Wrong

You know what we're talking about. Some days it just seems like everything goes wrong. It's a combination of all of those things that seem to happen on a daily basis that already keep you near the cliff of near insanity. All of a sudden, everything seems to begin to fall apart around you. You have equipment failures, your computer goes down in the middle of a transaction, or someone that you work with and depend upon calls in sick and you're left holding the bag. Then, you find yourself dealing with a series of difficult customers who seem impossible to make happy.

It can seem overwhelming. You want to run and hide, or you want to lash out to protect yourself; you want to "bite back" at the customer, or you want to just quit. You may feel vindictive and want to make the people around you "pay." You want them to get fired, to get reprimanded, or generally to not get away with it. It's stressful, it beats you down, you worry, and it causes you to lose sleep. Sometimes it can seem like there is no end in sight.

Unfortunately, there is no job or life that is free of stress, worry, and problems. At the same time, these issues become truly unfixable if you are unwilling to change or improve. Some people in fact hang on doggedly to the current situation. It's bad but at least it's familiar—and it might get worse. Change can be scary—sometimes even scarier than continuing to stay with an already bad situation.

Here is where your opportunity lies. We're not saying it's easy, but most times you can have a positive effect on your own circumstances. And, many times you can be a positive force for change in your work group and company as well.

Keep in mind that many people see themselves as "at effect" of the circumstances they find themselves in. You will sometimes hear this referred to disparagingly as choosing to be a victim of your circumstances. This phrase makes it sound bad and like it should be simple to fix. However, neither of these things is true.

## First, You've Got to Be Able to "See" That There Is a Problem

Many won't see the problem in the first place. That sounds silly, doesn't it? Of course I'll see there is a problem, right? Well, not so fast. Many of us have become so used to things being the way they are that it becomes normal. We increasingly fall into a pattern that becomes a rut, and eventually it becomes so familiar that we assume that's the way it is supposed to be. There are a number of things that can help you improve your competency at "seeing problems." It helps to broaden your perspective. Talk to other people who do what you do, participate in training programs, go to conferences, read business journals, and join and participate in professional associations dedicated to the improvement of your field. Take a class at a college, university, trade association, or community college. All of these avenues help you to gain perspective on how things are developing and improving. They also help you to see the difference between what is normal for you and what is normal for others in the world outside of yours.

## "Size Up" the Problem

Are you dealing with a situational or an infrequent problem that presents a challenge for you in the moment and isn't a regular occurrence, day after day? This doesn't mean it isn't frustrating, but if it is here and now and will go away, it is much easier to handle. In these cases, what's required is:

1. **Manage yourself and your emotions.** Separate yourself from the problem. Realize that you didn't cause it, but it's your job to help resolve it. Maintain appropriate perspective.

2. **Solve the problem.** *Listen.* You need to empathize with your customer without losing your perspective. At the same time, you need to skillfully get to the root of the problem, and look

for appropriate options for resolution. *Apologize*. Part of your ability to empathize includes being able to be sorry the customer is experiencing the problem and apologizing, even though you didn't cause it. *Acknowledge*. Connect with the reality that we may have contributed to this. Or, that this happens sometimes, and we're willing and ready to fix it. *Fix*. Offer the appropriate resolution and any accommodation you're able to and prepared to give him or her.

## Regular Occurrences, Patterns, and Never-Ending Cycles

Sometimes our equipment has glitches or isn't up to the demands of the job. Sometimes our processes are archaic or ineffective. Sometimes our employees aren't sufficiently trained, or aren't a good fit for the challenges of the job. This may show up as a pattern of frequent errors coming out of a particular step in the process, or a piece of our process that breaks down or slows down and is skill-related.

These obstacles are difficult to handle, even when you are in charge. When you are not the manager of these circumstances, it is even more difficult. Clearly, you can't fire the offending employee, go out and purchase new equipment or software, and unilaterally demand changes in your work processes or workflow.

In order to change and for improvement to happen at this level, you will almost always need to help your supervisor and manager engage and drive the change and improvement. It will usually require that person's:

- Knowledge.
- Understanding.
- Sign-off.
- Approval.
- Cooperation.
- Involvement.

So, what do you do? Here are a couple of things to keep in mind:

1. **Begin by managing yourself and your emotions.** Your ability to recognize a problem and recognize that you may be a contributor to it, but that it's bigger than your job, takes perspective and a seasoned attitude. It requires courage to confront it and play a part in improving it, particularly because some of your colleagues may be threatened by the attempts to change.

2.  **Be able to diagnose or help to diagnose the problem.** Your manager may not be close enough to the workflow or the systems you rely on to see that there is a problem. Or, he may be so close to it that he has difficulty seeing that there is a problem. It is essential that you have the capability to describe the problem in a manner that doesn't unnecessarily or prematurely assign fault or blame. You can only be a true Superstar customer service provider if you're willing to step outside of your narrow role and help to have a positive influence on the company's ability to serve your customers. These skills are included in our competency model presented in Day 7.

If you're willing to improve yourself and take initiative to do so, and you're willing to help your group and your organization to improve, and you do so, you can create a more effective level of service, and you'll create a better, more productive place to work for yourself as well. Some additional tips and ideas include:

- ▶ Resist the impulse to act hastily when under pressure.
- ▶ Keep from getting down in the dumps.
- ▶ Talk positively to yourself.
- ▶ Sort out what can be changed and what cannot.
- ▶ Find solutions to your most difficult problems.
- ▶ Break an upsetting problem down into smaller parts.
- ▶ Leave options open when things get stressful.
- ▶ Make a plan of action and follow it when confronted with a problem.
- ▶ Take your mind off unpleasant thoughts.
- ▶ Look for something good in a negative situation.
- ▶ Try other solutions to your problems if your first solutions don't work.
- ▶ Get colleagues or friends to help you with the things you need.
- ▶ Think about one part of the problem at a time.
- ▶ Visualize a pleasant activity or place.
- ▶ Pray, meditate, and/or get emotional support from community organizations or company resources.

| **Superstar Application** |
|---|
| 1. Overall, do you feel that your job experience on a day-to-day basis is mostly positive, neutral, or negative? What is it that most contributes to this feeling? |
| 2. Do you find yourself getting annoyed or stressed out with certain aspects of your job on a frequent, occasional, or rare basis? When there is an annoyance, what seems to cause it? |
| 3. Is there a skill, competency, or some particular knowledge that you could learn or improve and benefit as a result? What is it? And how and where might you acquire it? |
| 4. Is there a breakdown in your systems, processes, or people skills/capability that contributes to recurring problems in your job? How would you describe them without blaming or judging unnecessarily? |

| **Superstar Application (continued)** |
|---|
| 5. Who could contribute to fixing or improving these situations or circumstances? |
| 6. What steps might you take to bring the information to them in a helpful way? |
| 7. What should you avoid in order to minimize negative outcomes of such a communication? |

*If you work just for money, you'll never make it, but if you love what you're doing and you always put the customer first, success will be yours.*

—Ray Kroc

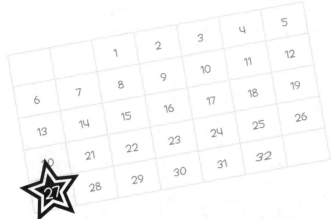

# How to Impress Your Boss
### *What to Do if All Else Fails*

How to impress your boss sounds self-serving, and it is. Let's get that straight. But, it's also about creating value and being valuable. The goal is not to be reliant on your boss or anybody else for your promotability and marketability. At the same time, it is rooted in the recognition that for every one of us, there are people out there who have an impact on our ability to influence, grow, and develop, and to expand a customer base that generates growth, stability, and, potentially, wealth. So, gaining and maintaining trust, credibility, and respect in your job is essential to your well-being.

The first thing to realize in this quest is that you need to distinguish yourself from the masses. It's much more common for you to work with colleagues who come up short in one way or another than it is for you to get a chance to work with fellow Superstars. Engagement scores are at nearly all-time lows. For the past few years, primarily because of the high unemployment rates caused by the recession and financial collapse, everyone has adopted the mindset that you are just lucky to have a job. Employees have been willing to put up with very difficult working environments and ridiculous expectations from many of the organizations doing business. Times have been tough, so it has been necessary to cut costs, and search for productivity and profitability everywhere it can be found. Many organizations have reduced their staff to ridiculously low levels, offered only minimal training for employees and managers, and have assumed a posture that says, "If you don't want to work in this environment, fine. There are many others right behind you who will gladly take this job if you leave." Employees are not stupid, however, and though they put up with these conditions, many seek to only do just enough to keep their jobs. Often their efforts fall far below what they are capable of. That's the nature of engagement. We all hold on to that reservoir of effort, commitment, ownership, and excellence that we can choose to expend on behalf of our employer, or we can quietly hold on to it and do what's required to meet the basic requirements of the job. What you should notice here is that the contract was changed on both sides of the employment equation, and for most of us, it's very obvious that excellence is rare. We hear it frequently from managers who are struggling with how to handle the many difficult situations they face on the job. In fairness to them, many of them have been dumped into a difficult situation with little or no training and huge staffs to manage, while they are expected to be in meetings from dusk to dawn. In our experience, employees who drive all bosses and all companies crazy are the ones who:

- ▶ Want and expect to do the "gravy" part of the job, but don't want to do the rest of it. These elements are the jobs that generate the most "positive press" (literally or figuratively speaking).

- ▶ Want the most comfortable aspect of the job, but don't want to do the "dirty work" or the parts of it that are done where it's hot, cold, dirty, smelly, early morning or late afternoon, and so on.

- ▶ Don't want to do the "crap work." Someone has to take care of the nastiest parts of any job, and these folks find ways to avoid it. This includes complex, tedious, hard work with heavy lifting or significant risk (physically or politically), and so forth.

- ▶ Complain all the time.

- ▶ Don't learn how to do different details that are essential parts of a completed, good job.

- ▶ Come in late; leave early.

- ▶ Abuse personal or sick time.

- ▶ Bother colleagues to get help with things that they haven't bothered to learn how to do.

▶ Brown nose, suck up, badmouth others, take credit for work that others have done, or instigate or contribute to the negative rumor mill.

▶ Lie to colleagues or to their supervisor/superior.

▶ Refuse to work with others, or expect others to carry their weight.

▶ Refuse to change, grow, improve, cooperate, take initiative, think, or step outside of the expectations they've built into their perception of their job.

That leaves a lot of room for Superstars to emerge. It is very possible to stand out in very positive ways in your job. Here are some basic operating guidelines for you to follow to move to the top of the heap.

## Give Eight for Eight

The first goal is to learn how to do your job and do it well. Carry your weight. And, if you carry a little more than what's yours to carry, so much the better. After all, your first job is to earn the money that you're being paid. Some of our early employers called it "eight for eight." It is a basic recognition and acceptance of a fundamental employment contract. You agree to pay me in exchange for doing work for you. We define the work and the role, and agree upon a wage for that work. If I do the work, you're obligated to pay me according to our agreement. If you look at the bulleted list in the last section, what you find is that a lot of your colleagues add addendums to the contract, or simply refuse to honor some aspects of the agreement. This becomes a management problem very quickly and conflict, blame, fault finding, argument, lack of trust, and poor teamwork quickly begin to show up in the workplace. If you, on the other hand, do your job—your complete job, including the hard, undesirable, or less-desirable parts, and the parts that others have a tendency to ignore, shrug off, or refuse—you immediately begin to stand out as someone who is easy to work with. We're not saying you should automatically step in and do all of the things that nobody else is willing to do without comment. But, if you do your share and your part without complaining and do it well, it will be noticed and appreciated by your boss. Yes, this includes making coffee when everyone else drinks it and leaves the coffee pot empty, or clearing jams in the copy machine even if your pay grade is way above that kind of work.

## Learn Your Job and Do it Well

Sounds like a no-brainer, but you'll be amazed how many of your colleagues don't know how to handle customer transactions that are an everyday expectation. Meet your deadlines and commitments; pay attention to your spelling, grammar, and punctuation in written documents; and cooperate with those who depend on you to do your work in order to do theirs. This also means to do all of your job, not just the parts that are easy, convenient, clean, conflict-free, and so on.

## Know Your Business: Keep Your Eye on the Big Picture

Even if you're in an industry that you don't plan on being in forever, you should know your business. How does this company make money? What do our customers want and expect from us? What are our products and services? How do the systems we rely on work to allow us to deliver?

It's what you do every day, so you may as well be the best at it. This includes knowing the industry. Keep your eyes open for new developments in your industry or business specialty. This awareness of the "bigger picture" gives you access to conversations about future opportunities or risks that affect the business. This knowledge and perspective translates into credibility and potential for future jobs or roles that require such perspective and personal initiative. So when a news story that covers your industry pops up in the news or in a professional journal, clip it and e-mail it to your team, boss included.

## Keep a Clean Workspace

Be organized and on top of your job. Whatever your workspace consists of, it is important for it to be organized and professional looking. It is a bit of a balancing act because you want your space to look worked in: not too cluttered, but not totally bare. If you have no paper or work tools on your desk, it doesn't look like you're working. But if you have no desk visible under all that paper, it doesn't look like you're working, either. Your disorganization makes it appear that your job is beyond your control. If the stuff you have out is that important, it's worth having it organized and usable. When you leave work for the day, take a few minutes to organize your workspace for the next workday. This is one of several places where the appearance takes on a bigger meaning than reality.

## Come In Early and Leave Late

Avoid that common tendency to get to work just before the time clock strikes "starting time" and having your keys in your hand, ready to go out the door when it strikes "day's over." Most bosses feel like you don't really want to be there, and that they're really getting taken for a ride instead of getting your best effort for the full day. An investment of another 10 to 15 minutes on each side of your day can pay off big time for you. If you're there and ready to start a productive workday 10 minutes before the clock hits start time, it's a whole different story. If you finish your day and begin to get ready to leave after the clock shows quitting time, your boss will see a whole different level of investment from you. That extra 10 to 15 minutes of your time each day will show a different side to your superiors. Instead of looking like you hate to be there and that you'll do anything you can to spend the least amount of time possible at your job, now it looks like you're an investment that's paying off. It also looks like you're excited about your job and, by doing this, you've just separated yourself from everyone else around you.

## Dress Professionally

The adage "dress for the job you want, not the job you have" is still a good rule of thumb. Look at the way the employees two or three steps up the ladder from you are wearing, and use that as your rule of thumb. If that is not appropriate for some reason, at least make sure whatever you choose to wear is clean, is neat, and does not draw negative attention in any way. Your appearance also speaks to your desire and capability to take on bigger responsibility for your job. Think bigger, look the part, and you'll stand out in a positive way.

## Look for Ways to Save the Company Money or Help Make More Money

Companies are in business to make money, simple as that. They do that in many ways, but the ability to get new customers and form long-term, loyal relationships is extremely important. The leadership of your organization is always looking for ways to sell more, cut costs, and make customers happy. Unfortunately, the higher they get into the ranks of management of the organization, the more removed they are from the day-to-day activities in the business. They miss things. They don't see all of the activities that take place in the business. Some procedures that should have been dropped or changed years ago continue, not because they add value, but because "that's the way we've always done it." Similarly, managers often don't see opportunities to satisfy customers that may appear to be "right in front of your eyes." Your constant search for these opportunities and your willingness to bring them forward as ideas for improvement can significantly help your transformation into the ranks of Superstardom.

## Form an Opinion and Share It

A result of all your efforts is that you may very well be asked for your opinion more frequently. When that time comes, don't be shy; it is to your benefit to offer it—even if it's in disagreement with one that others (including your boss) hold. If you can back it up with sound reasoning and facts, you will increase your credibility and value as an employee. Confident, reason-based opinion, even when it's a disagreement, has value, especially if you can accept that you still may be overruled. Your ability to accept a different direction and avoid argument will win you points as you demonstrate your value and seasoning.

## Come Prepared

Come prepared to do your job. Manage your attitude, and prepare yourself with the proper tools, knowledge, and information needed to perform without delay. Thinking about the expectations for each task and meeting you participate in gives you the opportunity to develop the mindset, and to plan and prepare to meet those expectations. Consistent preparation and successful task accomplishment result in achievement and advancement.

## Take the Initiative

This is a logical extension of several previous rules of thumb. As we discussed previously, many of your fellow employees look for ways to minimize effort and avoid unpleasant activity. If you seek responsibility, and take on and complete difficult tasks routinely, without complaint, and if you take on challenges that others avoid, and you solve problems without calling for help from your supervisor or manager, you demonstrate that you are the kind of employee who is capable of taking on and accomplishing more. The more you do, the more you'll be capable of doing. It is very rare that an employee is faulted or looked down upon for contributing more than expected or handling more difficult problems than others in that job. Do your job and do it well.

## Stay Marketable

The final recommendation we have for you in your quest for customer service Superstar status is manage your own career. Seek and maintain your skill level and ability to produce value, and don't depend on others to take care of your career. There was a time when if you worked hard, your company would give you a career for a lifetime and generally would take care of you as a member of the family. Today, we are all more or less "independent agents." In some situations, you will find that as long as you grow and produce, you will be rewarded and given the opportunity to grow with your organization. In other cases, however, the company will gladly accept the gift of your efforts and increasing value, but will not reward you sufficiently in exchange for the value you bring. In those cases, you're better off moving on to another organization that recognizes your value. It's a fine line today between moving when opportunity presents itself and the perception that you are a "job hopper." In the past, it was believed that having short employment stints (say, five years or less) was a reflection that you were unstable and couldn't be depended upon. Today, a five-year stay at a company may be a reflection that you've stayed too long. It is appropriate to keep your resume up-to-date continuously, and if you think you're being underpaid, test the market. You don't have to leave, but you'll always have the option if you take charge of your own career.

Bottom line: Do a good job, add value, manage your own growth and marketability, and be a Superstar wherever you choose to contribute.

| Superstar Application |
|---|
| 1. Build a list of your strengths and contributions as a customer service professional. What have you done to add value, and how has your company benefited? |
| 2. Build a list of your current skills and capabilities that make you a current or rising Superstar. |

| Superstar Application (continued) |
|---|
| 3. What are the next steps you plan to take to demonstrate your value and contribution at your current place of employment? |
| 4. What are your medium- and longer-term objectives for the development of your career? Identify the specific jobs or capabilities you plan to develop. |
| 5. Update your resume and online professional presence. Once you've developed your resume, complete an updated and complete presence on an online site such as LinkedIn or Google+. |

*Customer service is not a department; it's everyone's job.*

—Anonymous

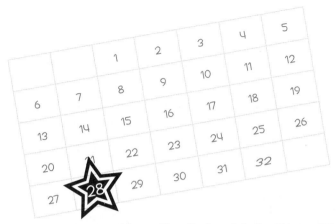

# How Do I Avoid Getting Stuck in a Rut?
## *The Power of Continuous Improvement*

We have all been there. Going to the same job every day, doing the same mundane tasks. Answering the same questions and working with the same people can leave us feeling a bit burned out and uninspired. Even the most motivated of employees go through rough patches and get stuck in proverbial "ruts." Ruts are not always easy to break out of. Sometimes simple things such as taking a break, getting fresh air, and trying to gain new perspective help, whereas other times nothing can seem to break you free. If you can avoid getting stuck in a rut altogether you can save a great deal of time and energy. A good way to avoid getting stuck in a rut is striving to continuously improve and develop the processes and services that make up your job, just like you're doing with this book. Striving for excellence and continuously improving not only will help in the road to success, but they also pave the way for you to become a Superstar.

There are many established continuous improvement models that lay the groundwork for the road to success. Each offers useful steps and many provide similar ways of getting from start to finish successfully. These steps include:

1. **Plan.** Define what you would like to improve upon, set measurable goals, develop strategies to meet these goals, and define measures of success.

2. **Act.** Take steps each day to set your strategies in motion and meet your goals.

3. **Analyze and evaluate.** Step back and analyze the results based on your measures of success. Define what worked and what should be done differently in the future.

## Plan

Planning is an integral part to successfully starting the continuous improvement process. When you are faced with the question of where to begin, it is best to identify areas of potential improvement. For example, let's say you are a grocery store supervisor and around noon every day there is an accumulation of customers at the checkout area and only one checkout open. Your employee or coworker at the check stand gets increasingly stressed with each additional customer joining the line and starts getting short with everyone, and your customers in line are getting more and more irritated. Meanwhile there are three employees restocking shelves and two more sitting at the customer service desk, each of whom don't seem to want to offer their assistance to their coworker. The issue in this scenario is clear; customers are getting upset, the employee at the front has more than his share of work on his hands, and no one seems to want to step in and help. After identifying the issue, ask yourself how the situation could be improved upon. Could you have someone stocking shelves go to the front and help? Could you funnel customers to the customer service desk to check out? Could you assign roles differently around this time of day to accommodate the rush of people? Chart out some goals and methods to achieve them, and then ask yourself, "What does success look like?" In this scenario, success may be less frustration shown by customers or customers getting through the line quicker. By defining measures of success, you will be able to accurately see if your actions worked or if you need to try something else.

## Act

After you have taken the time to plan out your course of action, it is time to set your plans in motion. Note that everything doesn't have to take place in one giant, sweeping change. It is just as useful to implement small steps every day to reach your goals. Start first by working on your check stand employee's communication with the customers. Ask him to take a breath and focus on the person he is helping, communicating with each person individually. When the customer gets up to the register, he should say, "Thank you so much for your patience," and when the transaction is complete say, "Thank you again and have a wonderful day." Encourage the employee to leave each customer feeling as if she were the only one in line and that she is appreciated as a customer and respected as a person. This small step won't solve the issue, but it will help address the larger issue at hand, which is customer dissatisfaction with the checkout process. By making each customer feel like his patience and understanding are acknowledged, and he is receiving great, polite service despite having to wait, it will leave him with a positive impression of the store. After taking this step, continue to take the other steps that you had planned in the following days or weeks. Perhaps you decide that in addition to better communication with the customers, you will give one of the employees stocking shelves the task of stepping up to the front to help when he or she sees a line is accumulating, or you yourself will go help. No matter what you do, taking steps to continually improve your processes and services will lead to a more successful workday.

### Analyze and Evaluate

Finally, after you have acted on your plans, take time to reflect on what resulted. Do customers seem happier as they leave the store because the employee at the check stand is concentrating on them instead of hurrying through their transaction without a word? Does the line move faster because you have given someone the responsibility to step up to another front register when the line starts getting long? Are people's impressions overall better than they were prior to enacting these changes? Observing the results of your actions is important to better determine what can be done in the future to improve or continue.

As you've learned so far, to be a Superstar customer service representative, it is important to be constantly learning and growing. Not only can it benefit your job prospects in the future, but it also helps you avoid getting stuck in those oh-so-familiar ruts that we all find ourselves in from time to time. By applying the continuous improvement model to your job, you will be able to clearly identify where improvements can be made and can strive to reach your goals. Not only will you impress your boss with your initiative but you will be able to catapult yourself into Superstar success.

> *Every company's greatest assets are its customers, because without customers there is no company.*
>
> —Michael LeBoeuf, author of
> *How to Win Customers and*
> *Keep Them for Life*

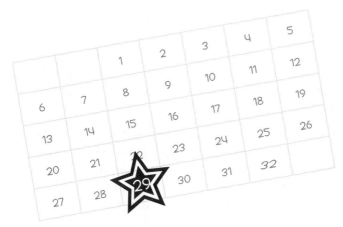

## Why We Need to Do More Than Just What It Takes to "Get By"
### Customer Service Is Everyone's Job

In your quest to improve yourself and become a customer service Super-star, it is helpful to consider the cultural habits of successful service organizations, such as Disney, Apple, Southwest Airlines, Wegmans, Nordstrom, and Amazon. These cultural habits are not merely lip service; they are proven ways of doing business and engaging customers. They involve the focus on all employees from the new hire, to the veteran, to the president of the organization. These cultural habits have helped these organizations survive and, more importantly, thrive in comparison to their competition. Each of the cultural habits here describes 1) examples of leading companies that are driven by customer-focused strategies, 2) the organizations' approach, and 3) the impact of each habit to help a company survive and thrive in an ever-challenging marketplace.

**Cultural Habit #1: Delivering a great customer experience is a way of doing business—not just a program.**

▶ Amazon's investor relations page states, "We seek to be Earth's most customer-centric company for four primary customer sets: consumers, sellers, enterprises, and content creators." Amazon put its stake in the ground by announcing its hope to be the world's most customer-centric company.

▶ Wegmans' motto is "Every day, you get our best." Wegmans makes grocery shopping a true experience rather than offering the same chore-like drudgery that most consumers expect at the grocery store. Its reputation goes well beyond its market area. In 2010, Wegmans reported that it received nearly 4,000 letters and e-mails from consumers in 46 states who urged the chain to open a store in their area.[1]

▶ Southwest Airlines began Love Field in Dallas. They became the "love airline" hiring attractive flight attendants and providing an entertaining flight experience. President Emeritus Colleen Barrett, has a favorite saying about Southwest Airlines: "We are a customer service company; we just happen to fly airplanes."[2]

▶ Apple's sales per square foot are higher than Tiffany and Co.'s. Apple employees are supposed to focus on helping customers, not selling products. A quote from the training manual demonstrates this commitment: "Your job is to understand all of your customers' needs—some of which they may not even realize they have."

▶ Disney cast members are taught an important truth: "The guest isn't always right, but let them be wrong with dignity." A secret to Disney's success is their guest-centered approach. Their philosophy is not just lip service; it actually guides behavior. Disney cast members consider what they do to be a helping profession and a noble calling.

| Application |
|---|
| What is the reality of your service to customers? How can you elevate your service? When will you do this? |

Companies who lead in customer service don't legislate it with policies and procedures; they live it. Employees routinely go the extra mile, and the stories shared within each of the companies become the standards to live by, deliver, and surpass. Employees want to do well because the leaders lead that way. Other companies have programs that become the "flavor of the month," devoid of inspiration and constantly changing without reason.

**Cultural Habit #2: Employee satisfaction and loyalty lead to customer satisfaction and loyalty.**

▶ Nordstrom's golden rule for employees is widely recognized: "Use good judgment in all situations." As Nordstrom demonstrates, top service companies are willing to trust employees, which gives employees confidence and satisfaction.

▶ Amazon's approach is to hire the world's brightest minds and to create an environment where they can invent and innovate the customer experience.

▶ Gary Kelly, President/CEO of Southwest Airlines, says, "While we fly planes, we are and always have been a Company of People, and they remain our greatest asset."[3] Southwest puts all prospective employees through a rigorous hiring process. New employees learn nine loyalty principles, some of which include: find the kid in everyone, do more with less, do what is right, and nurture the corporate family. At Southwest, employees are at the top of the priority pyramid; for this reason, Southwest focuses on delivering employees proactive customer service. Southwest believes that by doing this, employees will, in turn, spend their time trying to ensure the passengers, the second most important group of the pyramid, are getting great customer service, too.

▶ Employees at Disney are "cast members," not employees. People are never hired; they're "cast for a role." A strong Disney principle is that cast members should treat each other as they would a guest. The Disney formula for success is:

> "A quality guest experience + a quality cast experience + quality business practices = the future."

▶ Apple's Genius Bar employees are trained to say, "As it turns out…" instead of "Unfortunately…" in order to place a more positive spin on any bad news. If a customer mispronounces a product name or something else, employees are forbidden from correcting the customer. (Attention: Fry's, Best Buy, and any other retailer with an ego.)

This top-down cultural approach is a polar opposite to the ordinary bottom-up way of doing business. Instead of starting with the customer, it starts with the employee. Whereas other companies claim customer service is their top priority, their actions too often illustrate that shareholders and short-term performance really take precedence. Inevitably, their quality and service suffer because their goals and expectations aren't aligned with their employees; yet, they still don't seem to understand why they are failing.

| Application |
|---|
| What can you learn from this habit that's applicable to you? How can you work more effectively with your coworkers? What changes are you willing to make? |
| |

**Cultural Habit #3: Ongoing learning and development are integrated into the fabric of the organization.**

▶ Wegmans has an extensive employee-training program, and it's consistently listed as one of Fortune's "Best Companies to Work For." Training may have been a recession casualty in many places last year, but the budget for customer service courses at Wegmans increased in double digits over the previous year.

▶ Apple's meticulous attention to detail permeates the hiring process. Prospective employees generally participate in several rounds of competitive interviews, which assess various skills and attitudes. Once hired, employees are trained extensively in customer service, sales, and product knowledge.

▶ Walt Disney established the Disney University after opening Disneyland to use a structured learning environment to teach the unique skills that are required of Disney cast members. It was the first corporate university and remains one of the largest training facilities in the world. Numerous colleges and dozens of online courses provide a plethora of learning opportunities to employees and managers alike. Surprisingly, Disney University does not offer specific quality courses. This isn't an oversight. Instead, quality and service are built into all the training programs taught by Disney. In addition, the Disney Professional Development Program has trained 500,000 individuals from the public, in specialties like human resources, people management, and quality service.

| Application |
|---|
| At the end of this book is an overall action planning process. Commit to do it fully. Decide to be a customer service Superstar in attitude and behavior. |

**Cultural Habit #4: The customer experience is researched and measured, then the data is applied.**

▶ On the desk of Pete Nordstrom, the company's president of merchandising, sits a stack of letters from customers and employees, each telling a story about a memorable experience they had with Nordstrom. Few company executives can say the same.

▶ For years, Wegmans has used customer relationship management tools to gain insight into the customer wants, needs, and behaviors, so that employees can deliver better service.

▶ Apple doesn't have strict sales quotas in place for employees. It does have metrics like "attachment rates," the frequency with which staff members are able to provide customers with additional products like AppleCare. Those who fall short of the goals receive more sales training, which is really about helping customers with stated or perceived needs.

▶ One simple, effective technique used by companies like Apple is the "net promoter score." The net promoter score includes the number of customers who give you a 9 or 10 on a recommendation rating (promoters) minus those who rate you a 6 or lower (detractors). This approach provides a more powerful way of measuring a brand's effectiveness.

Compare these strategies to one $20 billion retailer that spends a few million dollars each year on customer surveys and mystery shops but has failed to improve. The company continues to lag in its industry in customer ratings, stock price, and profits. Customer-focused companies measure service and sales, sometimes in unusual ways, and then share and relentlessly apply the information to achieve better results. Their approach to business and culture demands improvement.

| Application |
|---|
| It is important to learn how well your company is doing in customer service. Ask to review all of your company's customer feedback data. How does this compare with other companies? (If you have this data. If you don't have any, find a partner to help you get this information.) What can you learn? How can you become more effective as a result? |

**Cultural Habit #5: Continuous improvement is expected, and the speed of gain is second to none.**

▶ The culture of Amazon promotes openness among all employees, which they believe inspires innovation. Their executive management supports this principle, which sets the example that employees then follow. Through this process, Amazon patented the one-click ordering technology, allowing customers to use previous payment information to order an item with a simple click. After its inception, shopping became easier because less thought and effort were needed. Jeff Bezos at Amazon also developed the notion of the "two-pizza team," which suggests that you can't feed one team with two pizzas because that's too much food. In business application, this limits the task force to five to seven people, depending on each person's appetite. This keeps the focus on innovating and executing the things that matter to customers.

▶ Disney's strong belief in attention to detail is what sets them apart from other organizations, priding themselves on having to "sweat the small stuff." Consequently, Disney pioneered the concept of exceeding people's expectations.

▶ Apple's Genius Bar is the in-store tech-support station. It's not a help desk or customer service center. The idea illustrates out-of-the-box thinking by recognizing employee potential and customer priority.

| Application |
|---|
| Make a commitment to go online and read or watch five other customer service articles or videos. Be open to new ideas. What can you learn or relearn? |

Each of the mentioned companies has been a leader in its respective field for some time. Their cultures ensure they have a sense of urgency to innovate and improve, so that they continue building customer loyalty. Because employees have freedom to act, they are able to deliver creative solutions at pivotal moments for each customer, which enhances each company's reputation and service delivery capability.

All of the mentioned companies have received many accolades from various sources, some of which include: JD Power, *Consumer Reports,* the American Customer Satisfaction Index, and *Fortune*'s "Top 100 Companies to Work For." Consistently, these companies shine in growth and profitability.

Many companies aspire to deliver the kind of service these companies do. Some try and improve while others try and fail. Most are unwilling to make the necessary changes because they lack the commitment and, more importantly, the ethics. At the heart of the matter what they really want is the reputation these companies boast, but they are unwilling to do the work it takes to earn it. However, any company that strives to improve by aligning these five cultural habits in its workplace will make a huge difference to the bottom line. Customer service Superstars have the ability to improve themselves and shine in customer service, regardless of where they work. *You* can, too.

> *You are serving a customer, not a life*
> *sentence. Learn how to enjoy your work.*
> —Laurie McIntosh

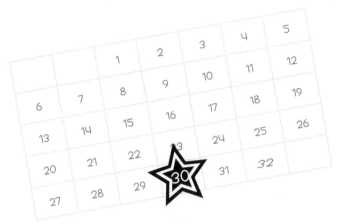

## Can Providing Good Service Take Me Anywhere?
### *Is It All Menial, Crap Work?*

Let's be honest: Some of your job responsibilities seem simply like crap work. Why, for instance, do you have to endlessly record how many hours you spent on making customer phone calls? Why do you need to continuously fill out expense reports that never seem to get turned in anywhere? Why do you need to continuously tidy racks that will only get shuffled around by customers? They may seem difficult to justify or to think of as anything that could possibly benefit you in the future, yet you are expected to do them and do them well. Fortunately, these jobs are not all for nothing. Though it may be hard to see at the time, they form the building blocks for your future career. To better understand why these parts of your job are important, you must first define why they matter, what they can bring you in the long run, and how to make them work for you.

Though some of your responsibilities seem insignificant, they lay the foundation for building the knowledge, skills, and mindset for your future career. Think of them as nails. They are tiny and almost completely forgettable when you look at the beautiful house that you have built; yet at the core they hold everything up. Without the nails, the house would fall down. With weaker nails, parts of the house would become unsteady. In the long run, you will find that many of the menial tasks that you were expected to do somehow infused something positive into your future career. Those racks you have to constantly tidy? They taught you to keep a clean, organized, efficient workspace. Those unnecessary PowerPoint presentations that you had to keep putting together to present to your boss? They taught you the value of good visual communication and helped you build skills to communicate effectively with upper management. Look at your job right now. What menial tasks do you have to do? What positive things can you glean from them? What skills do they teach that maybe you didn't recognize at first? It may not have been obvious right away, but when you look back, you will understand how these tasks were the building blocks for your future success.

Aside from building the skills and knowledge you need to succeed, these jobs show that you have personal and professional integrity. When you were hired, you were given a list of expectations, and you need to uphold your end of things and make sure they are completed. You weren't hired with the understanding that you will only do the fun parts of your job and the others will fall to the wayside; you agreed to do them all, good and bad. Take pride in the agreement that you made from the start and in turn take pride in all aspects of your job. They may not be glamorous, but if you give them a little more credit, you may actually find yourself enjoying them instead of dreading them.

Because these responsibilities lay the foundation for your future it is important to do them, and do them well. Challenge yourself to do these tasks better than anyone else and do them with a smile on your face. Your boss will appreciate your initiative and positivity, especially when you are doing things that everyone around you is dragging their feet on. If you and your coworker are doing the same task but you are doing it with positivity and enthusiasm and he is sullenly getting the job done, who do you think the boss will think of first when it comes to promotions and raises? Everyone wants to work with someone who keeps the environment positive, and these types of people climb the ladder much faster than their indifferent counterparts.

Now that we've discussed why these types of jobs matter, it's important to discuss the three key ways you can make them work for you.

1.  **Change your frame of mind.** You have a choice. You can look at things negatively or positively; they can be constructive or pointless, good or bad. It all depends on your frame of mind. Knowing this, it is time to stop looking at the "crap work" as just that. Instead, look at each job as an opportunity. It may be an opportunity to get a task knocked out quickly. You know what you have to do and you know how to do it, so get it done! The beauty of many of these jobs is that they are easy to

complete, so think of it as a mental break in your day. It may be an opportunity to apply new skills or a new approach that you have learned, in a work setting. Use these tasks as places to grow and test your skills, and build them for the future. If you can successfully take the negative connotations that come with these tasks out, you will find you can actually get them done better and faster, and get more out of them.

2. **Set goals for yourself.** Setting goals for yourself with menial tasks as well as the large responsibilities of your job gives you a tool to measure your skills and growth. Maybe it is your goal to get all of the little things out of the way by 10 a.m. so you have room for your bigger responsibilities for the rest of the day. When you go into work the next day, test out what strategies will help you get the job done by this time. Giving yourself goals and building on what you already do can help you develop new skills that you may have never had previously. The small tasks are a great opportunity to grow. Set goals for them and challenge yourself to get them done.

3. **Be present.** Throughout the day there are hundreds, maybe thousands, of things you could be doing at any given time. Sometimes you are doing multiple things at once. When you work this way, it is easy to think of your smaller responsibilities as nuisances instead of opportunities. To fight this, be present whenever possible. Do what you are doing in that moment and try not to think of other things. If you concentrate on the task at hand, you can get it done faster and move onto the bigger things that may matter more to you.

Sometimes, as the saying goes, it's hard to see the forest through the trees. When we are stuck doing menial tasks on a day-to-day basis, it can be tough to see how they fit into the bigger picture. However, it is important to recognize that you are being trained to become a better, more skilled individual and employee. By recognizing this, and devoting time to doing the tasks better than anyone else, you will set yourself apart for the rest and be able to realize your full potential.

> *We see our customers as invited guests to a party, and we are the hosts. It's our job every day to make every important aspect of the customer experience a little bit better.*
> —Jeff Bezos, CEO, Amazon.com

## Customer Service Slip-Ups: What to Do When It Isn't Working

We have told you about some amazing companies that have done everything right in the realm of customer service, going to what seems like the ends of the earth to please their customers and keep a loyal customer base. However, as you probably have deduced, this is unfortunately not the norm in the business world. Many more companies are guilty of bad customer service. In fact, every year *Forbes* and *Business Insider* dedicate lists to companies that are getting it wrong. It seems that, upon review, companies in every industry are guilty of treating their customers poorly. No matter if it is lack of communication, not listening, or just general mistreatment, some companies have become infamous for their customer service (or lack thereof).

### Long Island Power Authority (LIPA)

In recent years, LIPA has slipped an astounding 25 percent in customer service ratings by ACSI, going from 65/100 to 43/100 in just three years.[1] In addition to frequent complaints about unexpected rate hikes, poor communication, and unsteady reliability, it was LIPA's response to Hurricanes Irene and Sandy that garnered them the one of the lowest scores in ACSI history.

When Hurricane Sandy ravaged the East Coast, many residents were left without electricity in their badly damaged homes. According to an article in *Bloomberg*, 45,000 customers were left without electricity two weeks after the storm.[2] Inconvenient, yes, but what was worse was that residents were facing icy temperatures and snow storms post-Sandy, and the lack of power meant no heat for weeks in homes that sustained significant damage. During this time LIPA lacked even basic communication with its customers, gave inaccurate time estimates of when power would be back, and gave customers misinformation about when service crews would arrive. According to the *New York Times,* storm recovery efforts were made worse with outdated records systems including the use of paper maps to determine where storm damage had occurred and where power would be restored.[3] Days after the storm, LIPA's flawed online map at one point falsely showed that power had been restored to more homes in a town than were actually there in the first place. All the while customers were left rudderless not knowing when they would get electricity again.

Long Island Power Authority's response to Hurricane Sandy is a good example of how important it is to establish good customer service processes from the start. If better systems had been in place, and precautions had been taken to avoid these types of issues, the turnout may have differed greatly. With better communication with their customers, LIPA could have given more realistic time estimates and made a bad situation even slightly better. Instead, customers were left feeling neglected by the company that they depended on, and LIPA is left with a legacy of poor customer service.

## AOL

In 2006, it took one customer and a viral Internet hit to shine a light on AOL's poor customer service practices.[4] It was then that 30-year-old blogger Vincent Ferrari posted an audio recording of his efforts to cancel his five-year account with the company. During the conversation, where Ferrari asked to cancel the account numerous times, he was questioned time and time again by the customer service representative, who tried to convince him that he used the account enough to keep it. The account was finally cancelled after going in circles with the representative. However, the damage had already been done. The Internet lit up with thousands of other customers who complained of the same issue, a CNBC reporter tried to cancel his account and it took 45 minutes from start to finish. So, why was it so difficult to cancel your AOL account? Soon after Ferrari's post, AOL's "Customer Retention" manual was leaked online, revealing pages upon pages of strategies to get customers to keep their subscription with the company, a practice they dissolved in later years.[5]

As we have pointed out in previous days, listening is essential when it comes to customer service. One AOL representative's blatant disregard for listening to what the customer wanted, and instead creating an argumentative atmosphere, cost AOL more than just customers. The company sustained a large amount of negative media attention stemming from one customer's negative experience that other dissatisfied customers were happy to chime in on with their own experiences. What was a ripple in the negative media ocean became a wave. What should you glean from this? Customer's thoughts matter, and with the Internet and social media their opinions travel fast. It is important to make sure that your customer service practices are the kind that customers want to share with others because of their successes, not their failures.

## Transportation Security Administration (TSA)

Let's face it: Going through the security line at the airport is never a treat. However in recent years, the TSA has become known for little more than their customer service blunders. In May 2004 the TSA received a record high 4,027 complaints ranging in topic, from treatment at security checkpoints, lost or damaged luggage, and screening procedures. In 2010 alone, the TSA received 18,196 complaints relating to damage claims about checked bags.[6] When the TSA installed full-body scanners that gave revealing images of what passengers' bodies looked like, there was a national uproar. Everyone felt as if their privacy was being paraded around the airport for all to see with little to no care for what customers thought. Pair this with security checkpoints typically long wait times, in addition to personal items going missing during bag checks, and you have a recipe for a customer service disaster.

As a government agency, not much can be done if customers are unhappy; travelers have no alternative to the TSA. However, you have to ask yourself if you want your company to be known more for its poor customer service skills than the benefits you are providing a customer. The TSA is trying to make it safer for people to travel from one place to another, a noble job to be sure. But somewhere along the way it became less known for protecting people and more known for invasive, unfortunate, inconsiderate customer service. If that were the company that you worked for, is that what you would want to be known for?

Bad customer service abounds in the world today. The good news is, it doesn't have to. You have a choice: You can either provide exceptional service—the kind that keeps people coming back for more—or not. By reading this book you are taking a step in the direction of customer service excellence. Through applying the core strategies that we have discussed you can make the customer service experience second to none and truly become a Superstar.

> *Good customer service costs less than bad customer service.*
>
> —Sally Gronow, Welsh Water

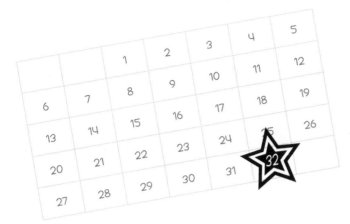

# Afterword: Action-Planning and Goal-Setting for Superstar Success

We know there aren't 32 days in any month. To finish, we want to do a quick summary review of the key points we've discussed with you, and the skills and concepts you've thought about and worked on to move forward with your development. Taken together, the concepts and thoughts on this 32nd day of your *Superstar Customer Service* journey should produce a launching point for the next stage of your career and life.

**Day 1: Beginnings Are Prophetic**

The reality is that all of us, in one way or another, are customer service providers. There is no role more important, and unless we do it well, it is unlikely that the business we work for will succeed. Your understanding of the importance of customer service and role is crucial to your success as an employee. Your results directly contribute to your company's reputation and success every day in winning and keeping customers. To be a Superstar customer service professional you will do your job with care, treating the external and internal customers with dignity, respect, and courtesy. You will also do a quality job in terms of the technical aspects of your job (data entry, correctness, completeness, quality, etc). Superstars excel in all aspects of what they do. If they don't know how to do something they ask for help, or learn it on their own. Over time they consistently outperform everyone else. We've learned that when we start well, there is a high probability that we will succeed in the end. Start with a solid understanding of what it looks like to be a Superstar, and chances are you will succeed in all aspects of your career.

### Day 2: What's My Job? What's Expected of Me? Why Am I Important?

We've seen it time and again. Lack of understanding of what's expected leads to poor performance. Whether it's at the front-line level of customer service or the senior management level, success begins with a clear understanding of what's expected of me. *Where are we going? What's my role?* and *What does an excellent job look like?* are three critical questions we must each understand the correct answer to in order to succeed. Superstardom comes from meeting and exceeding expectations.

### Day 3: How Serious Should I Be About This Work, Anyway?

Through time you will become "grooved into the track" of your job. Just like the wheels on a train track or the needle on a vinyl record, we follow the prescribed path that's set in front of us, and time seems to pass quickly and uneventfully. It's easy to give in to the sameness and succumb to the boredom that's often all around us. In this state, many of us fall into a willingness to give in to mediocrity and save our interest and passion for the time available to us outside of work. Is it any surprise, then, that we fail to strive for new growth and attempt to achieve the excellence that requires our focused attention, diligent practice, and continuous effort to provide value for our customers and our employer? It often takes more effort to manage ourselves than it does to do our job. Without the constant effort to try and to continuously improve, and to add value each and every day, you won't distinguish yourself from the other average employees around you. And, you won't achieve the potential that is available to only the Superstars among us. It's worth it. But it isn't easy. No one will remind you, and certainly no one will do it for you. You've got to get yourself ready, focus, think, do the work, serve your customers, and learn your business so you can do it better tomorrow, and still better the day after that. Excellence doesn't come easily or cheaply. Someone in your company will do it. Why not you?

### Day 4: What Does It Mean to Manage Myself?

Every manager dreams of having a team of employees who know what to do and do the job consistently with few problems. Often, what they find instead is a group of employees who don't want to be there, don't want to do the work, don't like the customers or one another, and act like sixth graders. We know this is harsh, but we can't tell you how many times we hear versions of this complaint from supervisors, managers, and executives. If you set high goals for yourself, determine exactly what your role and performance expectations are, and then work diligently to succeed and exceed those expectations, you will stand out. Guaranteed! If you can solve the problems that are presenting obstacles to your performance and help others around you succeed at their job with a minimum of drama and conflict, you will be a darling of your work group. If you can take it upon yourself to learn how to help the company make money, and delight your customers and coworkers such that they comment about the quality of your work on a regular basis you will become a Superstar. Your future will be yours to dream and create!

### Day 5: To What Standards Should I Try to Rise?

The bad news is that mediocrity passes for okay service in most service situations. Check it for yourself. How often are you amazed or even slightly surprised at the quality of service you receive out there? In this section you got a small dose of just how poor the state of service is. The good news that's what you're competing for. It's up to you, but our suggestion is to set high standards for yourself. Go for excellence! Be great and get ready to climb the ladder of success. You *will stand out!* This is the ticket to Superstardom!

### Day 6: The Difference Between Good Service and Superstar Service

In this section we define it for you. We point very specifically to the difference between good, regular, run-of-the-mill service and Superstar service. Excellence—when you see it you will know it. And, when you deliver it, your customers will know it. It's your choice. You're going to be there anyway so why not commit to a standard of excellence.

### Day 7: How Do I Currently Stack Up?

### Day 8: What Do I Need to Improve and Why?

Day 7 and Day 8 presented you with the competencies and assessment tools to take a clear-eyed view of your current customer service practices. You generated scores and had the chance to identify specific areas for focused improvement. Build that plan, use it to grow, and go back and assess yourself again. This is a path to greatness if you remain focused and disciplined about its application.

### Day 9: It All Begins With a Problem

It's the nature of the job. You're there to solve problems. You're there to accomplish difficult objectives, and you're there to help customers get satisfaction. If you're not skilled at managing yourself, managing relationships, and solving problems, you won't be successful. But, if you have mastery at these skills, the sky is the limit. It's always about a problem. Learn to deal with it, and it becomes about Superstardom.

### Day 10: What Would L.L. Bean Do?

You've probably already noticed that after the name of the chapter there is no further mention of L.L. Bean in this section of the book. We thought of them when we thought of companies with excellent reputations for providing customer satisfaction. That says something, doesn't it? We have included a few examples of other companies that consistently generate stories of excellence in their day-to-day business. We provided you with some guidance and tips to play your part for your company. We also encouraged you to manage your own career, and while doing your best for your company, we believe you also need to become your own career agent. Keep your resume and online credentials up-to-date and actively monitor and improve your career marketability. Your company will watch out for their best interests. You should watch out for your own as well. Being a Superstar is the basis for both. Go for it.

### Day 11: You Can't Treat Me Like That!

There are just some days where it seems like the people you're working with must be possessed by some evil entity. And, they often show up—or it seems they do, anyway—in bunches. One after another, people get angry, in your face, demanding, and downright rude. In this chapter, we discuss the dynamics of why this happens and what to do about it. We warn you that there are many times when there is no reason and there is really nothing you can do but bring your best to cope. But, we also discuss the important self-management requirements attached to your job. It's important not to miss the possibility that the rash of upset people may in fact be reacting to our own upset, frustration, anger or disgust. In other words, our customers and friends sometimes are mirrors of what they are picking up from us. Through learning to manage that, we can learn how better provide excellent customer service under any circumstance.

### Day 12: What You Should Expect From Your Boss, and What to Do When Your Boss Doesn't Do What You Expect

Communication, clear direction, training, coaching, guidance and support, an empathetic ear, a little understanding, recognition—is that too much to ask? Probably not, but we remind you that your supervisor can't read your mind, is pressed with meetings from dusk until dawn, probably hasn't done your job before, and may not (really) have a clue about how to train you or answer the specific questions you're grappling with. It's a big divide and is steadily getting bigger in most companies. You may luck out and get a good one. But, maybe not. What you can count on, though, is that if you want to succeed you need to find out what your job is and learn how to do it. Find somebody to help you answer those questions you don't know the answers to. Take the initiative to solve problems, and then let your boss know it's fixed and not to worry. Communicate your accomplishments to your boss on a regular basis. Let your boss know of any problems that may jump up and cause her or him difficulties. Bottom line: We're saying you need to step forward and make your situation work. *It doesn't matter* if your boss should have done a better job to help you if you let that cause you to lose your job or get a reputation as a poor performer or whiner. Life's a bitch; get used to it.

### Day 13: Begin With the Highest Form of Courtesy

You *"know"* this already, right? And, you probably think you're a good listener already. So, why is it that the people close to you tell you that you don't listen? And why is it that you miss details like start times, deadlines, procedure changes, addresses, directions, and so on? Listening is the most powerful and most underutilized influencing strategy available to any of us. It communicates loudly that you care and that you understand. It is the ticket to empower your problem-solving efforts, and to build long lasting and mutually beneficial relationships. But, you missed that last part because you really weren't listening.

One more time: You really need to be great at this if you're going to be a Superstar.

### Day 14: You're Going to Have to "Gotta Wanna" Lead Yourself to Success

One of the greatest challenges to achieving greatness is that point where we stop relying on outside motivation and support from our parents or our supervisors to motivate us, and we internalize the desire to do it for ourselves. The search for knowledge and the dedication to improving replace the drudgery of hearing someone else tell us what we have to do and how to do it. Along with that shift goes the willingness to be victim to other people's shortcomings. As soon as you realize that you are in charge, you stop blaming others for what's not working or not happening, and you stop relying on others to get you to success. It's a powerful place to work and live from.

### Day 15: Problem-Solving Your Way Through the Forest

You will be confronted with problems and barriers and obstacles that will make it difficult to achieve your objectives. The pathway forward often can be determined by clear thinking, cool demeanor, rational analysis, collaborative effort, and skillful negotiation. You've got to develop these skills.

### Day 16: Time Management

Seeing and hearing the realities around you put you "in position" to be productive. If you are mistaken because of your skewed perception of your circumstances, you will waste time and effort, and frustration and disappointment will be your most frequent outcomes. Learning to be productive is much more than just managing time.

### Day 17: Etiquette on the Phone, in Electronic Communications, and Face-to-Face

You have learned the top 10 mistakes we make when using the phone to conduct business and how to handle the phone professionally. We spend more and more of our time working with others who are not physically present. Using these tools effectively allows us to be productive and build strong customer loyalty even when we're separated by time, distance, and location.

### Day 18: How to Deal With That **ss***e

At some point in your career you will find yourself dealing with someone who is completely nasty and out of control. Others will know that it was the other person, not you, who was being ridiculous and unreasonable. He or she shouldn't have acted that way. Nevertheless, if you handle it badly, you run the risk of losing status, credibility, and or respect. Handle it diplomatically and graciously, and you stand to gain Superstardom. It's worth the effort and practice needed to develop the skills and confidence to handle this most difficult situation—whatever it is.

### Day 19: How to Say NO! Hell No! (Nicely?)

Satisfying customers is relatively easy when you're able to give them what they want. You can replace a defective product with a new, well-functioning one—or, you can meet their request for additional time or services to satisfy their needs. The difficulty is when they are unreasonable in their request or when they ask for something you can't or won't give. Handling the land mines of disappointment, anger, resentment, fear, and aggressiveness is a skill set that is essential to your success and to the success of your company.

### Day 20: How to Handle Complaints

Some customers and coworkers will be skillful and persistent in their quest for satisfaction. Some will be reasonable and others will get loud, go over your head, make a scene, embarrass and call you names, and the list goes on and on. Your success here depends upon your ability to manage yourself, the relationship, and having skill and confidence in your negotiation skills and techniques.

### Day 21: How Superstar Customer Service and Superstar Sales Go Together

You add credibility to your company's offerings. The most important service that a customer can receive is the benefit of having a knowledgeable, caring advocate who can help him or her get the best use from the customer's purchase. The value in a product or service is only available if the customer can be certain that he or she can make it work for the customer consistently and correctly. Day 21 is about building that trust one customer at a time. Building a trusting relationship, asking good questions, listening for understanding, maintaining focus on your customer's needs, making suggestions to meet those needs, and helping them make useful decisions. These are all skills that promote excellence in service—and they are also the essence of good selling skills. You do one while expertly taking care of the other.

### Day 22: Working With the Numbers

Part of mastering your job includes understanding exactly what's expected of you and how your performance is measured. If you understand it and can manage your success, you have the additional opportunity to zero in on those things that are most important, and you can avoid the distractions caused by things that, sometimes, just don't matter.

### Day 23: Surveys, Mystery Shop, Complaints, and Written Notes

Some of the most common measures are centered in surveys, mystery shoppers, and customer comments recorded through feedback mechanisms. These tools are often available to you in meetings and regular reports. They provide a great deal of insight into what works and what doesn't when working with the customers you're paid to serve. Knowledge is power. Learn about these reports, and follow them to chart your success as a customer service superstar.

**Day 24: You are Going to Hear About It, So You May as Well Make It Work for You, Not Against You**

The reality of working in any organization today is that there is a relentless effort to measure everything that matters, and use that information to drive out waste and improve productivity and profitability. Ignore these efforts at your own peril. On the other hand, learning about these systems and processes, and using them to master your job, often leads to great success in your job. You probably will be able to "get by" with a cursory knowledge. But, that is the point. Become knowledgeable and gain some expertise, and you may very well win a major advantage in the quest for excellence and career success.

**Day 25: Follow-Up Strategies and Going the Extra Mile**

Doing your job, finding ways to build relationships and ingratiate yourself to your customers, and going the extra mile are ways to separate yourself from the normal, everyday customer service providers. Remember that you need to look for opportunities to help, maintain an attitude that says, "It's my business to help," and listen to the little voice that says, "You should...." And then go ahead and do it. Make it your business to help.

**Day 26: What to Do When Things Go Wrong**

We sit in meetings regularly where the primary conversation is only about how "screwed up things are." We hear relentless complaining about how those idiots in other departments can't do their jobs right and we are always the ones who have to fix it. The computer is down and we've just got a new system update that isn't working right. We find ourselves wondering how any of these businesses make any money at all and how they even stay in business. We also find ourselves wondering why some of these employees don't quit, aren't fired, and so on. There is a lot of room for Superstars! Don't forget it. But, knowing it doesn't make it so. You've got to work on it, practice it, persist, and have long-term vision.

**Day 27: How to Impress Your Boss**

Eleven strategies for standing head and shoulders above the typical employees give you guidance for your job and career success. We also contrast these strategies with the mindless mediocrity that exists in almost every workplace in the world today. If you're not already shining as a standout customer service provider, it's not because the competition is that stiff. Take control of your life and your opportunities, and you can make it happen. It will not be handed to you, though.

### Day 28: How Do I Avoid Getting Stuck in a Rut?

There is always "more to go." Better is always possible. Climb to the top of the hill and you can more easily see what it will take to get to the top of the next one. Continuous learning and continuous improvement lead to the potential for excellence. It is interesting, can be exciting, and will result in a much more skilled, knowledgeable, and valuable you than doing what you've always done. Ruts and graves have a lot in common. Stay out of both as long as you can.

### Day 29: Why We Need to Do More Than Just What It Takes to "Get By"

The bottom line is that everybody doesn't get a trophy. Winners do. Not everybody will get a raise. People who have provided more in value than they've used up in cost do. Everybody doesn't get a promotion. Those who have demonstrated potential do. Customers don't respond well to everybody. They respond to people who care about them and demonstrate it, who help them solve problems and meet needs, who make promises and keep them, and who show respect for them even when they may not earn it. Tough job. Do it well and you'll stand out. Become excellent—a Superstar—and your customers and your boss will notice. You might go somewhere.

### Day 30: Can Providing Good Service Take Me Anywhere?

Let's be honest: Some of it is crap work. Much of it is not difficult or challenging. It doesn't matter what your field is, or your job; each has fundamentals and basics that hold up the important stuff. Fail to do the basics—the crap work—well, and nothing else matters. Great surgeons fail when very small germs escape sterilization efforts. Great bridges fall when small bolts evade maintenance. Do your job—all of it—and do it well. Excellence depends upon it.

### Day 31: Customer Service Slip-Ups: What to Do When It Isn't Working

It would be much more satisfying to end our journey with bright tales about all of the excellence that surrounds us in our businesses and governments and institutions. The truth is that, though there is much that's right and we're improving in many ways, we're still confronted with needs that outstrip our current capability to meet them. It seems that we can see much in hindsight. What "should have been done" that would have prevented the product failure or the human catastrophe that caused loss of life? We do those kinds of "postmortems" or "after action reviews." And, they help. The challenge is: How do we learn and improve before the breakdowns? How do we meet the needs as they occur? How do we maximize our potential in the heat of the battle? In this section, we take one more shot at making those distinctions. We hope that we can wake up to the potential and the need to work at it—continuously.

One of our friends and colleagues always ended each book and program with the challenge to take the next step and asking, "So what? Now what?"

We'll leave you with that challenge as well. Here are a few additional questions to ask yourself and steps to take to go the next mile in your quest for Superstar customer service.

1. What insights and learnings (or re-learnings) surfaced for you after reading the summary review of *Superstar Customer Service?*

2. What actions do you want to take to ensure your own growth and improvement in light of your learning?

3. Review your Superstar assessment and initial development goals (Day 7 and Day 8) to pick up your thoughts and ideas for development initiated there.

4. From whom do you need to seek support and guidance in order to maximize your developmental potential?

5. What is your next job or career goal as you progress with your career and personal Superstardom?

## Final Words: Going Where No Customer Service Star Has Gone Before

Good luck on your journey to greatness—to Superstardom!

Please go to our Website for additional resources:

▶ To purchase additional copies of *Superstar Customer Service* or any of our other books and training programs, go to *www. wcwpublishing.com.*

▶ To find copies of white papers, go to *www.wcwpartners.com.*

▶ To download material from our blogs, go to www.*wcwpartners.com/our-blog/.*

▶ To set up a consultation or retain us for a seminar, contact Doug or Rick at (888) 313–0514 or *info@wcwpartners.com.*

If you have questions that you would like to ask us, or if you have suggestions to products we might produce or books we should develop, you can address them to us at *info@wcwpartners.com.*

> *The customer experience is the next competitive battleground.*
>
> —Jerry Gregoire, CIO,
> Dell Computers

# Chapter Notes

### Introduction

1. Daum, Kevin. "10 Things Really Amazing Employees Do." *Inc.,* March 1, 2013. *www.inc.com/kevin-daum/10-things-really-amazing-employees-do.html.* Accessed June 1, 2013.

### Day 1

1. PIMS (Profit Impact of Market Strategy) data base of the Strategic Planning Institute. (PIMS is a database the researches business strategy effectiveness that publishes data this type of data. You gain access to the data with a subscription.)

### Day 4

1. Farber,  Barry, and Joyce Wicoff. *Break-Through Selling: Customer-Building Strategies From the Best in the Business* (Prentice Hall Trade, 1992).

### Day 5

1. "Man Saves Boy By Lifting Pipe From His Head." *Ocala Star-Banner,* November 2, 1980, page 3F.
2. "William James Quotes." Goodreads Website. *www.goodreads.com/author/quotes/15865.William_James.*

### Day 7

1. "Strategy Analytics: M2M Cellular Connections to hit 2.5 Billion by 2020." *Business Wire,* August 7, 2012. *www.businesswire.com/news/home/20120807006109/en/Strategy-Analytics-M2M-Cellular-Connections-hit-2.5.*

### Day 9

1. "75 Customer Service Facts, Quotes and Statistics." Help Scout, May 2012.

**Day 10**

1. "Why Zappos Pays New Employees to Quit—And You Should Too." *HBR Blog Network*, May 19, 2008. *http://blogs.hbr.org/taylor/2008/05/why_zappos_pays_new_employees.html*. Accessed May 25, 2013.
2. Beaudry, Jennifer Ernst. "Zappos Milestone: Customer Service ." *Footwear News*, 2009.
3. Colvin, Geoff. *Talent Is Overrated: What Really Separates World-Class Performers from Everybody Else* (Penguin Group (USA) Incorporated, 2010).

**Day 11**

1. Naisbitt, John. *Megatrends: Ten New Directions Transforming Our Lives* (Warner Books, 1988).
2. Hale, Roger, and Rita Machling. *Recognition Redefined.* (Tenant Company, 1992), p. 18.

**Day 12**

1. Ghaemi, Nassir. *A First-Rate Madness: Uncovering the Links Between Leadership and Mental Illness.* (Penguin Group (USA) Incorporated, 2012).

**Day 17**

1. "Voicemail." Wikipedia. *http://en.wikipedia.org/wiki/Voicemail*.
2. Internet World Stats. *www.internetworldstats.com/stats.htm*.

**Day 25**

1. Kruggel, Ben. "Ben's story: Going the Extra Mile." CNN, October 12, 2012. *http://ireport.cnn.com/blogs/ireport-blog/2012/10/12/going-the-extra-mile*.

**Day 29**

1. Pecor, David. "5 Surprising Facts About Wegmans." *Columbia Patch,* November 29, 2011. *http://columbia.patch.com/groups/editors-picks/p/five-things-you-should-know-about-wegmans*.
2. Aldridge, Blake. "Where Did Customer Service Go?" My Morning Commute Website, July 18, 2012, *http://blakealdridge.wordpress.com/2012/07/18/where-did-customer-service-go/*.
3. Southwest Airlines Website. *www.southwestonereport.com/2011/#!/garys-message*.

## Day 31

1. Benchmarks by Company, 2013. *www.theacsi.org/index.php?option=com_ content&view=article&id=149&catid=14&Itemid=214&c =Long+Island+Power+Authority*.

2. Dolmetsch, Chris. "Long Island Power Authority Sued Over Hurricane Sandy." *Bloomberg,* November 13, 2012. *www.bloomberg.com/news/2012-11-13/long-island-power-authority-sued-over-hurricane-sandy.html* .

3. Hakim, Danny, Patrick McGeehan, and Michael Moss. "Suffering on Long Island as Power Agency Shows its Flaws." *The New York Times,* November 13, 2012. *www.nytimes.com/2012/11/14/nyregion/long-island-power-authoritys-flaws-hindered-recovery-efforts.html?pagewanted=all*.

4. Wells, Jane. "How Hard Can it Be to Cancel an AOL Account?" NBC News, June 21, 2006. *www.nbcnews.com/id/13447232/#.Ud1xC47VBy4*.

5. Popken, Ben. "AOL Retention Manual Revealed." Consumerist, July 18, 2006. *consumerist.com/2006/07/18/aol-retention-manual-revealed/*.

6. Gumbrecht, Jamie. "How Much Do We Really Hate the TSA?" CNN. com, June 2, 2012. *www.cnn.com/2012/06/01/travel/tsa-complaints*.

# INDEX

# About the Authors

## Rick Conlow, CEO and Co-Founder

There aren't many who'd argue the fact that Rick is one enthusiastic guy. Even the titles of his books, articles, and training programs reflect his drive and positive energy.

A quick glance at his professional resume leaves you with the strong impression that effort and optimism are a winning combination. Case in point: With Rick by their side, clients have achieved double- and triple-digit improvement in their sales performance, quality, customer loyalty, and service results during the past 20-plus years, and earned more than 30 quality and service awards.

In a day and age where optimism and going the extra mile can sound trite, Rick has made them a differentiator. His clients range from organizations that are leaders in their industries, to other, less recognizable names. Regardless of their place in the market, their goals are his goals.

Rick's life view and extensive background in sales and leadership—as a general manager, vice president, training director, program director, national sales trainer, and consultant—are the foundation of his coaching, training, and consulting services. Participants in Rick's experiential, live-action programs walk away with a-has, inspiration, and skills they can immediately put to use.

These programs include BEST Selling!, Moments of Magic!, Excellence in Management!, SuperSTAR Service and Selling!, The Greatest Secrets of all Time!, and SuperSTAR Leadership! Rick has also authored *Excellence in Management, Excellence in Supervision, Returning to Learning,* and *Moments of Magic.* He and his business partner, Doug Watsabaugh, recently published with Career Press *Superstar Leadership, Superstar Sales,* and *Superstar Customer Service.*

When he's not engaging an audience or engrossed in a coaching discussion, this proud husband and father is most likely astride a weight bench or motorcycle, taking on the back roads and highways of the Unites States.

## Doug Watsabaugh, COO and Co-Founder

Doug values being a "regular person," with his feet on the ground and head in the realities of the daily challenges his clients face. His heart for and experience in helping clients deal with difficult situations distinguishes him from other sales performance and leadership development consultants.

His 35 years of experience as an executive coach and organization development expert make him a trustworthy, professional resource when you or your organization needs help. He has extensive knowledge of experiential learning combined with an acute skill at designing change processes and learning events, which has enabled him to measurably improve the lives of thousands of individuals and hundreds of organizations in a wide variety of industries, including financial services, manufacturing, medical devices, consumer goods, and technology.

Before starting his own business, Doug served as the director of operations for a national training institute and manager of organization development for a major chemical company, and was responsible for worldwide training and organization development for the world's third-largest toy company.

He was also a partner in Performance & Human Development LLC, a California company that published high-involvement experiential activities, surveys and instruments, interactive training modules, papers, and multimedia presentations.

Together, Doug and Rick have written eleven books on leadership, sales, customer service, and a variety of management topics. Doug has also co-authored two books with John E. Jones, PhD, and William L. Bearley, EdD: *The New Fieldbook for Trainers* published by HRD Press and Lakewood Publishing, and *The OUS Quality Item Pool*, about organizational survey items that measure Baldrige criteria. Doug is also a platinum level e-zine publisher, and he frequently contributes to the WCW Partners blog.

He is a member of the American Society for Training and Development (ASTD), the Minnesota Quality Council, and the National Organization Development Network.

Doug's father taught him the value of hard work, and it paid dividends. He funded his college education playing guitar and singing with a rock 'n roll band, experiencing a close call with fame when he played bass in concert with Chuck Berry. Not bad for a guy who admits to being "a bit shy."

Though Doug's guitar remains a source of enjoyment, it pales in comparison to his number one joy and priority: his family.

## Alyssa MacDowell, Communications Specialist

Whether designing a new layout or engaging others in conversation, Alyssa is guided by five core beliefs:

1. Optimism will take you anywhere. 2. Creativity is limitless. 3. Being open-minded to others' ideas and perspectives is essential. 4. Inspiration is everywhere. 5. Kindness and respect are vital.

Alyssa graduated with honors from the University of Minnesota in 2009 with degrees in Journalism (an emphasis in strategic communication) and studies in Cinema and Media Culture. While there, she worked on a diverse range of projects—from strategic communication campaigns to information design, graphic design and video production—all seasoned with her signature can-do attitude. Alyssa's optimism and exemplary work ethic earned her a spot into the Kappa Tau Alpha National Honor Society and Phi Kappa Phi National Honor Society. She was also a member of the Public Relations Student Society of America.

Alyssa's knack for communicating with people is a great fit for WCW Partners, but it's her strengths in graphic design, creative development, photography, film, and visual communication that make her much more than just a great communicator!

When she isn't working, Alyssa enjoys spending time with her family, traveling, cooking, learning different languages, studying photography, and writing and designing a cookbook. (And this is all in her spare time!)

# About WCW Partners, Inc.

WCW Partners is a performance improvement company focused on improving top line, sales, customer loyalty, and profits. We use nine key performance drivers to evaluate and help a company more quickly increase results and sustain them.

Based in Minneapolis/St. Paul, Minnesota, we work with clients in a variety of industries worldwide to help them excel in sales, service, and market leadership. We facilitate business growth and vitality through four practices: sales and customer retention improvement, organization and leadership development, innovation, and communications strategy.

## Who We Are

We don't mind telling you that we're different than most consulting firms you'll find in the marketplace. For one thing, it's our approach: When you hire us, you get us. But just as important, we're people who've had to wrestle with the same issues you have—how to strengthen sales, boost productivity, improve quality, increase employee satisfaction, build a team, or retain and attract new customers. To us, "We develop the capability in you" is more than a catchy phrase. It's our promise.

## Our Experience

Our clients include 3M, American Express, American Medical Systems, Amgen Inc., Accenture, AmeriPride Services, Andersen Windows, Avanade, Beltone, Canadian Linen and Uniform Service, Carew International, Case Corporation, Citigroup, Coca-Cola, Costco, Covance, Deknatel, Eaton Corporation, Electrochemicals Inc., Entergy, Esoterix, GeneralMills, GN, Resound, GrantThornton, Hasbro Inc., Honeywell, Interton, Kenner Products, Loews Hotels, Marketlink, Kemps-Marigold, Meijer Corporation, National Computer Systems, Northern Power Products, Parker Brothers, Quadion, Toro, Productive Workplace Systems, Red Wing Shoes, Rite Aid, Rollerblade, Ryan Companies, Schwan's Home Delivery, Target, Travelers Insurance, Thrivent, Tonka Corporation, and a number of nonprofit and educational institutions.

## Contact Us

To learn how you can do amazing things, visit us online for additional materials and resources that can help your development and that of your team at *www.wcwpartners.com* or *www.wcwpublishing.com*.

Contact Doug or Rick toll free at (888) 313–0514.